# BECOMING AN UNSTOPPABLE

# WOMAN

# ENTREPRENEUR

## 20 STORIES UNCOVERING
## BUSINESS GROWTH MINDSETS

# PART II

**HANNA OLIVAS & ADRIANA LUNA CARLOS**

ALONG WITH 18 TRAILBLAZING
WOMEN AUTHORS

ISBN: 978-1-960136-58-9

# Table of Contents

# INTRODUCTION

She Rises Studios was created and inspired by the mother-daughter duo Hanna Olivas and Adriana Luna Carlos. In the middle of 2020, when the world was at one of its most vulnerable times, we saw the need to embrace women globally by offering inspirational quotes, blogs, and articles. Then, in March of 2021, we launched our very own Women's Empowerment Podcast: *She Rises Studios Podcast.*

It is now one of the most sought-after women-based podcasts both nationally and internationally. You can find us on your favorite podcast platforms, such as Spotify, Google Podcasts, Apple Podcasts, IHeart Radio, and much more! We didn't stop there. Establishing a safe space for women has become an even deeper need. Due to a global pandemic, women lost their businesses, employment, homes, finances, spouses, and more.

We decided to form the She Rises Studios Community Facebook Group. An environment strictly for women about women. Our focus in this group is to educate and celebrate women globally. To meet them exactly where they are on their journey.

It's a group of Ordinary Women Doing EXTRAordinary Things.

As our network continued to expand, it became clear that there was an urgent necessity to offer guidance and empowerment to women facing insecurities, uncertainties, fears, and various other challenges within the realm of entrepreneurship.

**Becoming An Unstoppable Woman Entrepreneur - Part 2: 20 Stories Uncovering Business Growth Mindsets**

Welcome to "Becoming An Unstoppable Woman Entrepreneur Part 2: 20 Stories Uncovering Business Growth Mindsets," where the transformative journeys of twenty exceptional women unfold, revealing the secrets to entrepreneurial success. Within these pages, you'll embark on an inspiring adventure through the success and tribulations of these trailblazing women who have defied the odds to achieve greatness in the business world.

As you explore their captivating stories, you'll discover the power of growth mindsets and the transformative techniques that propelled these women to stand out amidst the chaos of the entrepreneurial landscape. Each narrative is a testament to resilience, determination, and the unwavering pursuit of success.

From overcoming seemingly insurmountable challenges to seizing every opportunity that came their way, these women offer invaluable insights and lessons learned from their entrepreneurial journeys. Their stories serve as beacons of inspiration, motivating readers to embrace change, cultivate resilience, and unlock their own potential as unstoppable entrepreneurs.

Get ready to be empowered and motivated as you embark on a thrilling quest to make a lasting impact in the ever-evolving world of business. Whether you're a budding entrepreneur, a seasoned business owner, or simply seeking inspiration, "Becoming An Unstoppable Woman Entrepreneur" offers a wealth of wisdom and guidance to support you on your path to success.

Join us as we celebrate the courage, tenacity, and innovation of these twenty remarkable women. Their stories will resonate with you long after you've turned the final page, igniting a fire within you to become an unstoppable force in your own entrepreneurial journey.

Prepare to uncover the growth mindsets and strategies that will propel you towards greatness. Your journey to becoming an unstoppable woman entrepreneur starts now.

**She Rises Studios offers:**

- She Rises Studios Publishing
- She Rises Studios Public Relations
- She Rises Studios Podcast (FREE to Listen to!)
- She Rises Studios Magazine
- Rise with Hanna Olivas - Featured on FENIX TV
- She Rises Studios Community Facebook Page (FREE to Join!)
- She Rises Studios Academy
- KNOWN SRS
- FENIX TV

We won't stop encouraging women to be Unstoppable. This is just the beginning of our global movement.

**She Rises, She Leads, She Lives…**

With Love,
HANNA OLIVAS
ADRIANA LUNA CARLOS
SHE RISES STUDIOS
www.sherisesstudios.com

## Adriana Luna Carlos

Founder and CEO of She Rises Studios & FENIX TV

https://www.linkedin.com/in/adriana-luna-carlos/
https://www.facebook.com/adrianalunacarlos
https://www.instagram.com/sherisesstudios_llc/
https://www.sherisesstudios.com/
https://www.srslatina.com/
https://fenixtv.app/

Adriana Luna Carlos is an accomplished web and graphic designer, author, and mentor with a passion for helping women succeed in life and business. With over 10 years of experience in graphic and web arts, Adriana has built a reputation as an innovative leader and entrepreneur. In 2020, she co-founded She Rises Studios, a multi-digital media company and publishing house that has helped countless clients achieve their branding and marketing goals. In 2023, she co-created FENIX TV, an online streaming platform that showcases stories of people breaking barriers, shattering stereotypes, and triumphing against the odds.

As an advocate for women's success, Adriana challenges her clients and mentees to strive for nothing less than excellence. She has a deep understanding of the insecurities and challenges that women often face in the business world and provides the guidance and resources needed to overcome them. Her success as a business leader and entrepreneur has made her a sought-after mentor and speaker at events around the world.

Through her work, Adriana has demonstrated a commitment to creating opportunities for women to succeed in business and life. Her passion for innovation, leadership, and women's empowerment has made her a respected figure in the business community, and her impact will undoubtedly continue to inspire and empower women for years to come.

# MENTORSHIP AND DIVERSITY IN ENTREPRENEURSHIP

By Adriana Luna Carlos

Setting big dreams is not just about envisioning a distant future; it's about creating a roadmap for your entrepreneurial journey. As an unstoppable woman entrepreneur, take the time to clarify your vision and define your goals with precision. Consider what success looks like to you—whether it's launching a thriving startup, scaling your business globally, or making a positive impact in your community. Embrace the power of visualization and create a vivid mental image of your desired outcomes, anchoring yourself in the belief that you have the capacity to achieve them.

In the previous chapters, we explored the power of dreaming big and making our realities even bigger. Now, it's time to channel that energy into becoming unstoppable women entrepreneurs. In this chapter, we'll dive into practical strategies to unleash your entrepreneurial potential and pave the way for success in the business world.

Turning dreams into reality requires more than wishful thinking; it demands strategic planning, focused action, and unwavering determination. Begin by translating your big goals into actionable steps, breaking them down into manageable milestones that you can tackle one by one. Develop a comprehensive business plan that outlines your mission, target market, competitive analysis, marketing strategy, and financial projections. Pay meticulous attention to detail, anticipating potential challenges, and devising contingency plans to mitigate risks along the way. Remember that entrepreneurship is a journey of continuous learning and adaptation, so remain agile and open to refining your approach as you progress.

## The Power of Resilience

Entrepreneurship is inherently fraught with uncertainty and adversity, but it's your response to setbacks that ultimately determines your success. Cultivate resilience as your greatest asset, drawing strength from past experiences and using failure as a catalyst for growth. Embrace a growth mindset that views challenges as opportunities for innovation and learning, rather than insurmountable obstacles. Surround yourself with a support network of mentors, peers, and allies who can offer guidance, encouragement, and perspective during difficult times. Practice self-care and prioritize your well-being, recognizing that resilience begins from within.

Looking back at each moment and how I overcame impossible situations and adversities, I see new growth and amaze myself. Each life event created new outlooks and built my strength and resilience. I found a voice when I was most afraid to speak up and defend my honor. I followed my passion even when others may not have believed in me. I never allowed myself to be complacent in stagnant moments, but rather, pushed through life's resistance and continued to fight for the outcome I desired. People can unintentionally make you doubt yourself, but you MUST trust your capabilities and fall back on yourself. Always set boundaries for yourself and others because if you don't, you will only be living for others. If you can keep finding all the ways to train your mind to be strong, you will achieve an unstoppable mindset. Steps on how to make your dreams big and your reality even bigger Start by setting big dreams and understanding why it's important to never settle for less than what you truly desire. Understand that dreaming big is a great way to increase motivation and achieve your goals. Understand why it's important to make your dreams a reality by taking actionable steps. Write down the importance of setting realistic goals in order to reach bigger dreams. Understand the value of being organized when trying to make your dreams come true. Understand how staying focused on your goals can help you reach them faster. Understand the importance of not giving up, even when things get tough—"keep pushing forward"! Understand that having a positive attitude can help you achieve your wildest dreams!

It's important to dream big and make sure nothing holds you back from reaching those dreams. You should always strive for your best potential and never settle for less than what you deserve. Becoming An Unstoppable Woman Entrepreneur Means: Invest in your education by taking free courses or attending free seminars to help you learn more about personal finance and investing. Doing so will not only make you more knowledgeable but also more confident when it comes to making decisions with your money. Take a free class at a local college or university. You can find classes that teach money management, budgeting, and home buying. There are so many FREE resources around us that have value. So before you purchase that next course, research an alternative or watch a YouTube video on the same topic. Extract as much information as possible; that way, you can see what information you are still missing. Another way to invest in yourself is by developing positive money habits. This includes budgeting, tracking your spending, and setting financial goals. By managing your finances effectively, you will be better equipped to weather any financial storms that come your way. I often see individuals purchase a new product or service and not pay attention to the fact that they are spending more than they are making. Then at the end of the month, they realize they cannot afford their purchase. Take the extra time to plan and see where "investing" makes the most sense according to your budget.

## Building a Support Network:

Building a strong support network is essential for navigating the ups and downs of entrepreneurship with confidence and resilience. Seek out mentors who can offer wisdom, guidance, and valuable insights based on their own experiences in the business world. Join entrepreneurial communities and networking groups to connect with like-minded individuals who share your passion for innovation and growth. Cultivate relationships with peers and allies who can provide emotional support, accountability, and collaborative opportunities. Remember that entrepreneurship is not a solitary endeavor; it thrives on the collective strength and support of a vibrant ecosystem.

## Embracing Innovation:

Innovation lies at the heart of entrepreneurship, driving progress, differentiation, and sustainable growth. Embrace a culture of innovation within your business by fostering creativity, experimentation, and bold ideas. Stay abreast of emerging trends, technologies, and market opportunities, remaining agile and adaptable in your approach to business development. Encourage a mindset of continuous improvement among your team members, empowering them to question the status quo, challenge conventional wisdom, and pursue innovative solutions to complex problems. Embrace failure as an inevitable part of the innovation process, viewing it not as a setback but as a valuable learning experience that informs future iterations.

## Empowering Others:

True success as an entrepreneur is not measured solely by personal achievements but by the impact we have on others and the legacy we leave behind. As unstoppable women entrepreneurs, let's use our platform and influence to empower and uplift those around us, especially fellow women striving to make their mark in the business world. Mentorship is a powerful tool for fostering growth and development, so seek opportunities to share your knowledge, insights, and experiences with aspiring entrepreneurs. Champion diversity and inclusion within your organization, recognizing the unique perspectives and talents that women and underrepresented groups bring to the table. Collaborate with like-minded individuals and organizations to amplify your impact and effect positive change on a broader scale. By empowering others to realize their full potential, you not only enrich their lives but also contribute to a more equitable and inclusive society.

## Celebrate:

Celebrate all the moments, big and small, because they all matter equally. Allowing yourself to accept and celebrate even the smallest of achievements gives you a sense of accomplishment and the confidence to move on to the next goal in your life. I believe in positive reinforcement, and it promotes a healthy mind. Find Your Passion, Find Your Purpose, and Persevere! Reframe your limiting beliefs and celebrate all the small and large milestones in your life.

Becoming an unstoppable woman entrepreneur is not just about building a successful business; it's about realizing your full potential, making a meaningful impact, and inspiring others to do the same. By setting big dreams, taking decisive action, embracing resilience, nurturing relationships, fostering innovation, and empowering others, you pave the way for your own success while creating a ripple effect of positive change in the world around you.

In conclusion, never be afraid to dream big and take action. You deserve happiness and the opportunity to share your passion and purpose with others. So, find your passion, set ambitious goals, and persevere through challenges. Reframe your limiting beliefs, celebrate every achievement, and empower those around you. With an unstoppable mindset and unwavering determination, you have the power to turn your dreams into reality and leave a lasting legacy as a successful woman entrepreneur.

## Hanna Olivas

Founder & CEO of She Rises Studios
Podcast & TV Host | Best Selling Author | Influential Speaker |
Blood Cancer Advocate | #BAUW Movement Creator

https://www.linkedin.com/company/she-rises-studios/
https://www.instagram.com/sherisesstudios_llc/
https://www.facebook.com/sherisesstudios
www.SheRisesStudios.com

Author, Speaker, and Founder. Hanna was born and raised in Las Vegas, Nevada, and has paved her way to becoming one of the most influential women of 2022. Hanna is the co-founder of She Rises Studios and the founder of the Brave & Beautiful Blood Cancer Foundation. Her journey started in 2017 when she was first diagnosed with Multiple Myeloma, an incurable blood cancer. Now more than ever, her focus is to empower other women to become leaders because The Future is Female. She is currently traveling and speaking publicly to women to educate them on entrepreneurship, leadership, and owning the female power within.

# BE YOUR OWN $HERO

By Hanna Olivas

This book was created for all women who want to be their own financial $hero. Women around the world face many different forms of financial issues and struggles.

This book will teach you not only how to survive but to thrive as a single mother raising children and wearing all the hats. You deserve abundance and more. Your children depend on you, so let's show them how a boss mom does it!!

To the wife who may be facing divorce or financial bankruptcy: there is a way to overcome it and be financially fit again or for the first time.

For the college student who is drowning in student debt loans: in this book, you will learn how to break free and plan for an amazing future ahead.

For the grandmother who wants to retire, travel, or just spoil her grandkids: this book gives you the strategies and empowerment to do it all.

To all the ordinary women who are doing extraordinary things: this book is for you and will give you all the tools and guidance needed to be your own $hero!

Being your own $hero requires bravery, strength, inspiration, education, and celebration. It requires your vision and a clear understanding of who you are and where you want to be. Create the life you want to live, not the life you want to run from. When we say the words money, debt, budget, or finance, we tend to cringe unless we are a woman who is completely and financially fit. I believe no matter where we are in life, we, as women, can always learn more and do more to better ourselves and our finances. Your first step toward becoming an unstoppable financial woman is to:

1. Evaluate

- Mind, body, soul, health, wealth, etc. See where you are currently and be honest.

2. Discover

- This part is exciting and so important. This is where you discover what you want!

3. Create

- Once you have evaluated your life and finances and discovered what you want, it is time to create. This is where you develop a plan. Be realistic in your plans and goals. Also, be realistic with your to-do list! Don't overdo it, or you will burn out!

4. Execute

- By this step, you have already evaluated, discovered, and created your life's financial plan. Now it is time to execute and take action.

**Things you may need for this:**

a. A mentor, coach, or advisor

b. Educate yourself on financial fitness

c. Be diligent and consistent.

d. Have Faith in the Process

e. Acknowledge and reward your achievements, no matter how big or small.

f.  Form your financial dream team, which should include banks, advisors, and anyone else who can empower and inspire you to be your own $hero!

Keep going; seek knowledge; share advice, and live a financially fit life. Continue to be unstoppable in your financial journey. This is your time to make $hit happen. This is where you learn your true feminine financial power.

Let's talk next about other types of wealth.

1.  Health
2.  Mental Health
3.  Time
4.  Relationship

All 4 of these need to be aligned to be unstoppable.

If one is out of balance, it's only a matter of time before they are all out of balance. Prioritize each one in a manner where they can all connect.

Here are a few quotes I can always share:

*"What good is your wealth without your health?"*
—A. Finkelstein

*"She Rises, She Leads, She Lives"*
—Hanna Olivas

*"Time is the wisest counselor of all."*
—Pericles

*"An investment in knowledge pays the best interest."*
—Benjamin Franklin

So you see, ladies, money is one part of life's gifts, not all. I hope that you will look deep within and learn to be your own $hero.

## Victoria Stakelum

The Success Smith
Psychologist & Success Mindset Specialist

https://www.linkedin.com/in/victoriastakelum/
https://www.facebook.com/victoria.stakelumwassmith
https://www.instagram.com/thesuccesssmith/
https://thesuccesssmith.com
https://thesuccesssmith.passion.io

After a first career in corporate leadership and business growth consultancy, Dr Victoria Stakelum is now a multi-award winning psychologist, Success Expert and NLP Master Coach – she specialises in how to harness the power of your subconscious mind to make more brilliant things happen in your business, career and life!

Victoria's toolkit is a broad and unique one spanning energy healing, emotion release and regulation, success mindset, transformation and manifestation.

Underlying all of her methods is a belief that in order to Succeed, you must first Heal. Victoria has supported hundreds of clients to create alignment within themselves and unlock extraordinary performance and success. By releasing the negative emotions and limiting beliefs that keep them in procrastination, struggle and unmanifested potential, Victoria helps her clients heal their self-worth and confidence wounds, enabling them to develop the skillset and mindset to achieve fulfilment and success in relationships, business and life.

# UNLOCKING YOUR SUCCESS MINDSET: A BLUEPRINT FOR FEMALE ENTREPRENEURS

By Victoria Stakelum

In the fast-paced world of starting your own business, there's a tough reality that every hopeful entrepreneur faces—a truth that's taught in business classes everywhere. Sadly, this reality hasn't changed much since the 1990s, which doesn't paint a very positive picture for those who want to dive into entrepreneurship.

Here's the disappointing fact: most new businesses don't make it. About 10% of them shut down within the first year, and by the fifth year, that number jumps up to around 50%. After 15 years, a whopping 75% of startups have failed. It's clear that while the journey of being an entrepreneur is exciting, it's also incredibly tough.

Success in entrepreneurship isn't just about knowing your stuff or having a good product or service. It's about having confidence in yourself and being able to overcome challenges—a mindset that's especially challenging for women entrepreneurs. Women often struggle with self-worth, imposter syndrome, and a tendency to shoulder excessive burdens to please everyone - sometimes at the cost of their own well-being.

Navigating my own journey to becoming a successful woman in business has taught me that mindset is absolutely key to success. Whether coping with failure, creating personal effectiveness or inspiring high performance in others, a 'success mindset' is not just beneficial, but essential.

In this chapter, I will share practical strategies, and actionable steps to help you master your mindset and empower you on your entrepreneurial journey. We'll explore the secrets to going from hesitancy and self-doubt, to becoming an unstoppable woman entrepreneur.

Allow me to introduce myself—Dr. Victoria Stakelum. After 20 years in corporate leadership, I pursued a second career in psychology, NLP Coaching, and emotional healing work, relocating to rural Ireland to align with my deepest passion and purpose – risking, but not sacrificing, security and financial abundance. My journey involved learning to follow my heart, master my mindset and conquer my fears. And as it turns out, I wasn't alone...

In October 2023, I had the privilege of joining 17 remarkable female entrepreneurs in a month-long working retreat in Gran Canaria. Connecting with these extraordinary women, I discovered common threads weaving through their ambitions and vulnerabilities—the interplay of Love and Fear in their narratives and the pivotal role of mindset in creating aligned, successful outcomes.

## Cultivating a Success Mindset:
## A Journey from Fear to Love

Across the expanse of human experience, just two forces hold the power to propel us or keep us stuck: Love and Fear.

If you want to succeed in any human endeavour – including creating a successful business - you need to know how to tap into LOVE, and release yourself from FEAR.

A mindset fuelled by love is a game-changer. It connects you to a deeper resilience, resourcefulness, and passion, facilitating smoother navigation through challenges and quicker rebounds from failures. It magnetises relationships and opportunities to you and becomes the driving force that propels you forward, even in the face of adversity.

On the other hand, fear can be a formidable obstacle, manifesting as self-doubt, imposter syndrome, and a reluctance to take necessary action. Fearful lives and businesses are laden with struggle, indecision, friction, and stress.

As women entrepreneurs, this dynamic takes on a unique significance, shaping the very fabric of our professional journey.

Fostering loving alignment as a woman entrepreneur is a transformative step toward unlocking your full potential. It is not just about our mission, but about embracing the belief that there are limitless opportunities, resources, and success to go around. This contrasts with the fear-based mindset, which operates from a place of lack and limitation and can even manifest itself in physically debilitating symptoms that limit our ability to thrive. Coming from love allows us to view the universe as abundant, understanding that we are supported, worthy and that our success doesn't diminish the success of others or make us less lovable. Embracing this perspective opens doors to a wealth of opportunities, collaborations, and creative expression, propelling your business to new heights.

## The Fear Within

During my time in Gran Canaria, fear was like an uninvited guest at our entrepreneurial party. Even these super-successful high achievers, selected for their vision, potential, and brilliance, felt the weight of fear at every turn.

Fear whispered "I am scared of what the future will hold if I screw up," "I am scared of giving up my job and focusing on this full time," and "I am scared of failing." Fear found a home in resistance to releasing control —"I am scared of putting too much pressure on my team," and "I don't want to delegate in case things go wrong." Imposter syndrome echoed with "What if I'm not good enough?" and "What if I can't do it?" Fear was like a sneaky shadow, slowing us down, causing stress, and draining the joy from our journey.

This fear wasn't confined to business challenges; it seeped into personal spaces too. Whether it was fear of swimming in the ocean, walking in unfamiliar areas, or driving to new locations, fear had woven itself into various aspects of our lives.

## Combatting Fear

Liberating ourselves from fear involves a conscious effort to challenge our self-constructed narratives and instead seek evidence of what might be possible. A good place to start could be to ask yourself "What would I do if I had no fear".

By acknowledging the things you avoid due to fear, you begin challenging yourself to take action more aligned with your desired outcomes. However, our minds are adept at justifying stories that support our fears. Once we decide something is true, we seek evidence to reinforce that belief —a psychological phenomenon known as confirmation bias.

**Seek contradictory evidence**: Like a great big 'echo chamber' or the algorithm on social media, the part of your mind responsible for what you notice (it's called the Reticular Activating System or RAS for short) - will keep giving you more of the same messages that you have already decided are 'true'. But you can bring conscious awareness to this and change it.

Challenge the prevailing beliefs that fuel your fears. For example, Instead of accepting that "women encounter unique challenges such as gender bias and limited access to resources," seek evidence that "women create greater success because of their natural skill in communication and engagement ." Gain inspiration from the narratives of successful female entrepreneurs, learning from their experiences, challenges, and triumphs. Notice how readily you can find examples of what is possible when you actually go looking for it.

**Ask yourself, "What could go right?"** When starting a business, you're bombarded with decisions—investment choices, marketing options, hiring dilemmas, and prioritization challenges – you become a decision making machine! Fear, a natural human emotion meant for protection, can, at times, become a hindrance. This built-in negativity bias—a survival mechanism rooted in our early evolutionary development – leads us to focus more on risks and failures, which can block action and create indecision - potentially devastating for your business.

It's essential to recognize when fear becomes a barrier and take proactive steps to either release or confront it. Try embracing "No lose decision making." When confronted with multiple options, intentionally concentrate on the potential benefits and upsides of each, creating a list of possible positive outcomes. Shifting focus in this way helps cultivate balance, clarity, and courage, enabling you to overcome fear and take decisive action.

**Embrace Failure as a Stepping Stone:** Shifting your perspective on failure lets you learn, adapt, and evolve. Renowned entrepreneurs like Oprah Winfrey and JK Rowling faced early career failures. They show us that failure isn't an end point but a stepping stone on the journey to success. Adversity is an opportunity to adapt and build resilience. So instead of fearing setbacks, see them as valuable lessons. Use curiosity as your shield and superpower. Curiosity opens up possibilities and allows you to take responsibility by learning and moving forward . A success mindset believes there's always more to discover. Instead of self-blame, ask, 'What is there to learn?'

Fear may seem omnipresent, but empowerment begins with acknowledging and tackling it.

## The Power of Love

Love emerged as a recurring theme among the women entrepreneurs I came to know and care for in Gran Canaria. We are not talking here about romantic love, but rather the kind of deep passion that comes with finding your calling or discovering your mission. Many entrepreneurs embark on ventures that make logical sense based on their skills or experience, but lack a deeper sense of alignment or connection. When the inevitable challenges of early stage business growth come up, it is easy to give up. "Maybe this isn't worth it". "I'm not sure this is what I want to do". The lure of returning to stable employment pulls.

My own journey reflects this dynamic. I started a strategic consultancy back in 2013. It was financially successful but I just didn't love it! By 2015 I had decided to return to employment. Contrast this with my current business, which is much more focused on people than projects, and on energetic alignment rather than profit. I truly LOVE what I do now and it generates effortless abundance. I wouldn't return to employment in a million lifetimes, no matter what challenges I faced! Loving what you do becomes a driving force that propels you through fear, providing the resilience needed to weather the storms.

One of my fellow entrepreneurs faced numerous challenges during our retreat, but her unwavering emotional investment in her business's larger purpose eliminated any thoughts of giving up or changing direction.

If fear is your constant companion, taking bold steps becomes a formidable challenge. Conversely, a business born out of love and purpose has an inner momentum that always prevails.

## Connecting to love

The cliché of finding and embracing your 'why' holds profound truth and is perhaps the most important aspect of building your business. Pursuing your true mission instils a natural determination and resourcefulness, a conviction that you will find a way because you feel called to do so. Consider the story of Sara Blakely, the founder of Spanx. Sara approached her entrepreneurial journey motivated by deep passion and purpose – to help women feel confident and comfortable. Today, Spanx is a globally recognized brand, illustrating the motivational power of passion and purpose.

## How to create your business from LOVE

- **Use love as your compass**: In pivotal decisions, ask, "What would love do?" Let this guide you, steering clear of fear, self-judgment, or others' expectations. Don't let your fear masquerade as a sensible voice of reason - learn to tell the difference between your fear-voice or inner critic and that deeper wisdom and intuition that guides us. If you struggle to know the difference between these two voices, a great technique to use is to spend 5 minutes in quiet contemplation. If, in this calm, expansive mindset, the voice urging you forward gets louder, listen to it. It is likely guiding you to alignment and purpose. If however, from this calm, grounded space, your positivity diminishes or the discouraging voice grows, you are probably on the wrong track. To avoid letting insecurity drive you to adopt others' approaches; learnt to connect to and follow your heart. By staying true to your path, you will build an energized, aligned and successful business.

- **Find your tribe**: One of the joys of running your own business is that you get to choose the people you work with. Be selective, have fun and build your team, customers and clients to be people that you really vibe with so that every moment of your business life is filled with joyful connection, understanding and fun, rather than misalignment, stress or frustration. This takes courage and the ability to say no, which can be daunting in the early stages of business growth. But it is a vital step in maintaining alignment. You may also need new skills around how you hire, communicate and delegate, so make sure that you.....

- **Invest in yourself**: Success is not a destination; it's a way of being. Allocate time and resources for continuous personal development. As a female entrepreneur, your ability to adapt and learn is what will set you apart. The investment you make in yourself directly contributes to the success of your business and to your enjoyment of it. Remember, <u>you</u> are your most valuable asset.

- **Love yourself** - In the whirlwind of entrepreneurship, prioritize self-compassion and care. Your mental and emotional well-being is crucial amid the demands of business. Embrace practices like mindfulness, movement, and self-reflection for a balanced life. Self care enhances emotional stability and in turn improves decision making and judgement. Let go of perfection, strive for balance and treat yourself with kindness, as you would a friend. This fosters a positive and nurturing mindset, essential for long-term entrepreneurial success.

- **Come from abundance**: Fear often limits our ambitions, keeping us small. To foster abundance, we must emanate success energetically. Expressing gratitude, even for minor gifts, not only nurtures a positive outlook but also attracts positive energy. Spend moments daily visualizing your flourishing business, immersing yourself in the emotions of already having achieved success. Recognize and celebrate even the smallest victories, as these fuel your journey. Abundance extends beyond personal success; it involves cultivating open-heartedness through collaboration. Being receptive to partnerships unlocks unexpected opportunities and guidance. A supportive community can facilitate connections that buffer you as you navigate the unpredictable ups and downs of entrepreneurship. This communal support was the most profound and enriching aspect of my experience with fellow female entrepreneurs in Gran Canaria.

## Mindset Mastery: A Key to Success

We have explored how the emotional and energetic makeup of the entrepreneur mindset is the true predictor of business success. The journey to success requires a transformation from fear to love. Fear, if unresolved, hampers visionary clarity and courageous decision-making, impeding business prosperity. Conversely, aligning with your work and embracing love fosters motivation and vital energetic influence, connecting you to abundance and infinite possibilities.

The Success Mindset is an active choice, positioning female entrepreneurs as creators of abundance, testament to the entrepreneurial landscape's inherent goodness.

Most of us require some support to help us embrace a Success mindset, whether that's about releasing fears and limiting beliefs, learning to feel worthy enough to prioritise self-love or discovering what our deepest passion and purpose may be, so that we can pursue it.

For guidance, visit The Success Smith website to learn more about how I can help you release fear, overcome limiting beliefs, and discover your true calling.

As you embark on this journey, let love be your compass, fear your stepping stone, and success your inevitable destination.

If you're hungry for more insights, strategies, and a personalized roadmap to success, I invite you to connect with me. Together, we can unlock your full potential, pave the way for success on your terms and redefine what it means to be an unstoppable woman entrepreneur.

Written in loving memory of Barbara Nerć-Szymańska, President of ISACA Warsaw Chapter and Fellow of the Break Gran Canaria Cohort October 2023

## Samantha Pasley

CEO and Founder of Kismet Enterprises, Tipsy On Tap Inc, iPos Inc, Pasley Family Contracting, öra Permanent Jewelry

https://linktr.ee/samiam625

I am a serial entrepreneur who loves passing out smiles, reaching goals, helping to change lives, following my gut, taking risks and showing other women they have the opportunity to live the life they deserve while loving every minute of it.

# LET YOUR PLATE OVERFLOW

By Samantha Pasley

Hi, my name is Samantha Pasley, and I live in the beautiful state of Maryland. I'm a mother of five and a serial entrepreneur, to say the least. In this chapter, I'm going to share my journey of becoming an unstoppable woman entrepreneur who not only manages the responsibilities of motherhood and running four businesses but also how I draw strength and motivation from my Marine Corps background. This chapter will explore the importance of pursuing my passions, embracing multiple roles, and encouraging women to fill their plates with all of the things they love and enjoy. I will share insights, strategies, and practical advice to empower women entrepreneurs who are balancing their entrepreneurial endeavors, motherhood, and personal interests.

By harnessing the valuable skills I acquired as a Marine, I quickly learned persistence, discipline, and resilience pay off when you keep pushing towards your goals. Those traits have helped me to become the wife, mother, partner, businesswoman, and leader I am today.

At a young age, I knew that I wanted to be my own boss. I had no idea what entrepreneurship was, but what I did know was that I wasn't afraid to put in the work in order to achieve the goals I set for myself. Unfortunately, college was just not for me. My brain felt like it was constantly running at full speed and coming up with new ways to make money while incorporating the things I loved to do. I struggled with sitting in a classroom and focusing on one subject. I also struggled with the thought of doing one job for the rest of my life. The problem was that I have always been interested in so many things, and I've always wanted to fill my plate with everything that I love. I couldn't fathom the thought of having one career path and doing the same thing for the rest of my life when there were just so many things I wanted to do.

Starting a business is scary though. How was I supposed to be a mom and wife and equally provide for my family? I was determined to learn how to make it work and make it work fast. It definitely comes with its struggles, especially in the beginning. You have to get into a grove and create a routine that allows your business to fit into your lifestyle and your lifestyle to fit into your business. By no means was it or is it easy to find balance and prioritize my responsibilities on a daily basis. One thing I pride on is that I value my time and worth very much so it makes scheduling my days a lot easier. Understanding the importance of time management and organization is going to be a key factor in running one or one hundred companies. Luckily, there are so many apps and templates to help individuals do both. Sometimes you just have to play around with more than one to see what fits your lifestyle. Personally, I'm the queen of checklists. I love to use the notes section on my phone and I find so much satisfaction in checking things off of my list every day. When it comes to my schedule, there are always going to be non-negotiables. Those are always my family activities and anything having to do with self-care. Those two things will always be a priority in my life and my business. Everything else will find a way to my calendar and fit in around them. I think that it is essential to leave space on your calendar for those moments when life throws you a curveball. As women in business, we have to learn to be flexible yet disciplined when it comes to our calendars.

Sometimes, maintaining a healthy work-life and home life can be stressful. Trust me, I get it. However, finding a happy balance will allow for things to flow a lot more smoothly and allow for a higher vibration in both areas of your life.

I've found that surrounding myself with like-minded individuals and mentors has always played a key role in how my businesses evolve and become as successful as they have been. If you are a control freak (like I am), you probably have a hard time delegating tasks to others, but there comes a time when you need to let your guard down and pass the baton. Not only for your mental health but also for the simple fact that you can't do everything alone all of the time. It's impossible and just not realistic. Sometimes, you need to hire that VA or pay someone to run your social media accounts. When you identify the things that you are good at and work on them, then assign the things you are not so good at to someone that IS good at them, it allows you to enjoy what you do more and more every single day. See, the moment you stop loving what you do is the moment it's time to reevaluate or move on to doing something that brings you joy again.

And that right there is how my journey as an entrepreneur began. As a young mother, it just never made sense to me why I was waking up and going to work from 9 to 5 in an office, Monday through Friday, just to pay for my children's daycare. I was missing out on so much of their lives and missing special moments I wanted to be a part of and experience with them.

One day, it all just clicked. I realized that I could be the mom I always wanted to be and still make money and help support my family without having to work in an office all day long for someone who dictated my schedule and salary. I quickly came up with ideas and strategies that were going to help me enjoy and embrace motherhood while using my creativity and resources to produce a stable and steady income.

I started to learn about direct sales and joined multiple companies where I never really felt like I was part of a team and didn't have any success. I actually felt like I spent more money than I made, and therefore it left such a bad taste in my mouth. The best part for me about being in direct sales was that I got to network and get out of the house from time to time, hang out with a bunch of fun women, and host parties. And if I went home with a couple extra bucks in my pocket, it was even better.

I quickly learned that I needed to add something else to my plate that would bring in more money and satisfy more of my desire to do things that I love. I opened an indoor educational play place for kids with a friend of mine and was able to enjoy every moment of the day with my children while getting paid. It was a win-win on so many levels. Sadly, that came to an end a few years later, and it was back to the drawing board for me.

Even though my business eventually failed, I learned so much about entrepreneurship and the importance of community. It never felt like I failed because of all of the self-growth and knowledge I was able to take away from the experience. I met so many incredible people within my town and learned about so many other women who had the same desires, but feared the unknown when it came to becoming an entrepreneur.

One of the most significant things that I learned about myself throughout my first entrepreneurial experience was how fulfilling it was for me to be able to empower other women. I decided that I wanted to focus more on my direct sales business at the time because it allowed me the most flexibility with my family's schedule and the possibilities for growth were endless. Fast-forward 11 years, and I'm still in the same industry, helping to empower women so they can live the life they deserve. However, breaking societal stereotypes and embracing multiple roles has always been a huge challenge for me. Many people speak down on women in MLM companies and immediately label us as "scammers." However, I like to say the reason that they speak down on women like me is because they just don't know what they just don't know.

Direct sales has been around for many, many years, and although it has been given a bad reputation, it has also opened the doors for many women to be able to stay at home or work remotely while raising their children and playing an active role in the lives of their family all while earning and contributing financially. Had it not been for the company I am involved in, I'm not sure I would have grown to become the entrepreneur I am today. The day I joined and became a brand promoter, I was negative $16.47 in my bank account, my home was in foreclosure, and my car was on the verge of being repossessed. I still took the leap of faith and joined the company because in my gut I knew that this product and opportunity would help change the lives of so many women that would in turn change MY life.

I very quickly reached the highest rank in the company, earned every milestone achievement offered, and topped it off by becoming one of the company's first-ever seven-figure commission earners. So, I guess you could say that the bad taste that I had in my mouth was no longer a problem. One of my life goals is to inspire others to pursue their dreams fearlessly with passion and drive as if failure is not an option. I get to do that on the daily now.

I have since started three more companies that satisfy my desire to be creative and serve others. Each company has taught me so much about business and the industry that they are in, but most importantly, they have taught me so much about myself. They have shown me my inner strength. They have humbled me at times when I needed it most. They have broken me down and built me back up to be stronger and smarter. They have challenged me and defeated me only to prepare me and reward me with more success. They have proven to me that it's OK to fill my plate until it's overflowing. But most importantly, my experiences have shown me that filling my plate with things that I love allows me to enjoy my life more and not always feel like I'm working to survive.

In conclusion, my story of becoming an unstoppable woman entrepreneur, mother of five, multiple business owners, and a Marine Corps veteran is a testament to the immense strength, resilience, and determination that women possess. By embracing your unique background and skills, finding balance, nurturing a supportive environment, overcoming challenges, and encouraging women to pursue their passions, you can create a fulfilling and successful entrepreneurial journey. Remember, it is possible to fill your plate with all the things you love and enjoy while making a positive impact on the world. Your story serves as an inspiration to women everywhere, showing them that they too can achieve their dreams and excel in multiple areas of their lives. Be YOU. Be RELATABLE. Be HAPPY.

## Monica Marrone

Eco-Wellness
Health Coach | Author | Speaker

monicamarrone.com

My mission is to inspire you to become your healthiest self so you can best serve God and others. My motto is to Be More, Make More, and Give More.

My holistic approach to health - Living Younger Longer is about not letting your age define who you are, what you are capable of doing, and who you are becoming. It's about approaching the world with the same fascination and delight we had as children. I strive each day to be an example of this Living Younger Longer lifestyle.

When I'm not in the kitchen exploring healthy recipes, you might find me running a half marathon, facilitating a women's group at church, or leading a group of women hiking the Grand Canyon. I shared my story of faith and fidelity in marriage in the face of mental illness, addiction, and co-dependency in my debut as a published author in You Can You Will.

# BE MORE, MAKE MORE, GIVE MORE

By Monica Marrone

Everyone has a different path to becoming an Unstoppable Woman Entrepreneur. Woven into my story of transitioning from employee to entrepreneur are the accumulated lessons and skill sets that have brought me success and enriched my life. I hope you uncover some wisdom for your journey.

"I'm going to lose my job today!" I was on my phone with my husband on my way to a meeting for all salaried employees. He was in denial that I could get fired after 19 years of loyal service. At the meeting, it was announced that the company was eliminating 200 salaried positions, and they gave us directions to go to our office and wait for a phone call. I called my husband again and delivered the message one more time as I was certain my name was on that list.

Sure enough, I got the call, and I was summoned to a meeting with the young woman who was the head of the department I worked in. I could tell that she was nervous about delivering the news. My job was being eliminated. She expected me to be upset and start crying. She was startled when I cracked a big smile. I gladly signed the severance paperwork, accepting the package they offered me. I saw it as my ticket out of the corporate world and into the land of entrepreneurship, which was the direction my heart was leading me toward.

I decided that day that I never wanted to rely on the whims of corporate America for my entire income again. Although they told me they were eliminating my position, the reality was that they hired someone else to do my job at a much lower salary. I didn't want to be a part of that system any longer. I was determined to be successful in growing my own business in the health and wellness network marketing industry, but I was also naive about what it would take. I had little to no experience running a business!

For over 20 years, my career in the creative industry was not only our family's primary income; it was my identity. I was an art director in the catalog industry. I was an employee. I got a paycheck. I had a work schedule. I was discarding that role for my new title business owner.

This longing to be free from the confines of a job had been evolving ever since my son was born. For many years, I loved what I did. I got to travel around the world, and I worked in an interactive team setting that suited my creative and social spirit. Then, my reality changed when my son was born. Leaving my eight-week-old baby in daycare to return to a full-time job was heart-wrenching. And I found that my job was changing too. Due to new management, the fun, interactive parts of my job were disappearing. I was sitting in a cubicle, stuck in front of a computer all day, unhappy and unfulfilled. I realized then that I didn't want to do this for the rest of my life.

The desires in my heart were to have more time with my family, to focus on being healthy and active, and to have a positive impact on people's lives. I embarked on this journey with enthusiasm, purpose, and passion, but not much in the way of knowledge and applicable skills.

The transition from employee to entrepreneur requires a different mindset, and in my case, a totally different skill set. I floundered the first few years and wasted a lot of money on advertising. I read a lot of books and attended many conferences and workshops. I learned many concepts along the way about having a positive mindset, being determined, and knowing your "why"… But my first big breakthrough in really understanding what I needed to DO to grow my business and reach a level of competence and success came when I started studying the behavior of successful people.

## Skills for Success

I had a big "Aha!" moment when I realized that everyone I knew who was successful in my industry and life, in general, had three key skill sets:

1. They asked a lot of questions.
2. They told a lot of stories.
3. They mastered the art of inviting.

I set out to master these skills, and my business began to grow. And I was having more fun, too! These three skill sets are still the foundation of what I do. It might sound overly simplified, but these are the keys to success.

## Asking Questions to Build Relationships

One of my mentors, Eric Worre, boils it down to "All Business is Conversation" (ABC). The best way to engage in conversation is to ask a question. We are programmed from an early age to answer when we are asked a question, but the first response is often only at the surface level. I learned about the art of continuing to ask questions in a non-threatening way to get people to open up. There is power in asking open-ended questions. "How," "What," "Where," and "Who" are powerful tools to put into your question toolkit. "Why" is not as effective because it often causes people a level of discomfort. An effective conversation is one where the person you are conversing with does most of the talking! You often will not get to the person's reality until you go through three to four rounds of questions. An effective way to keep the conversation going is to say, "Tell me more about that."

Many years later, I was reintroduced to this skill set while attending the Institute for Integrative Nutrition's Health Coach Study Program.

They call it "High Mileage Questions."

By asking questions, you are affirming the other person. You are showing interest in them and valuing them. In our busy society, people often are surrounded by other people but seldom get someone's focused attention.

"They may forget what you said, but they will never forget how you made them feel." Said notably by Maya Angelou, among others.

I sometimes challenge myself to brush up on my question-asking skill set while I'm out in public. I've engaged people in retail stores and restaurants, while traveling, and while hiking trails. Are you up for the Conversation Challenge? See how long you can engage a perfect stranger that you meet in public in a conversation.

## The Magic is in the Stories

I first realized that telling stories is critical to success by observing people. Over the years, I have attended so many workshops and trainings around this topic that it's hard to rightly credit all the people I have learned from.

By sharing your story, telling other people's stories, and speaking in stories, you will find that doors and hearts will open. Stories engage people's imagination, and they will remember a story much more than they remember facts or scientific information. It's through our stories that we connect on a deeper level, sharing our struggles and triumphs in a way that resonates with others.

Here are the four components of a compelling story:

- The "Before"—the pain or challenge that was present in our lives. This could be a moment of doubt, a period of struggle, or a significant obstacle that seemed insurmountable.

- "What Changed"— the pivotal actions, decisions, or realizations that set us on a new path. This is where the transformation takes shape.
- The "Results Received" — the outcomes of our journey, the tangible and intangible rewards that came from facing our challenges head-on.
- "Inspiration and Call to Action for the Audience" — to engage them, to reflect on their own stories, and to consider what they can change to achieve their desired results.

By sharing our stories, we not only grow personally but also build rapport with our audience. I've found the saying, "People do business with people they know, like, and trust," to be so true.

My business began to grow sustainably when I adapted my approach from telling people facts about the products I was endorsing to asking questions and sharing stories.

## The Art of the Invitation

People like to be invited rather than told. I've found inspiration in Seth Godin's ingenious philosophy of seeking permission from potential clients. Permission marketing isn't about inundating potential clients with unsolicited messages; instead, it is a strategic and respectful approach that extends a courteous invitation to "take a look." When you fully embrace the concept of permission marketing, the art of inviting emerges as a subtle yet critical skill set that propels unstoppable women entrepreneurs to new heights. This method has allowed me to cultivate meaningful relationships founded on trust, mutual interests, and understanding. As my mentor Frazer Brookes explains business, it's, "Turning Strangers into Friends, and Friends into Family." My ability to turn perfect strangers into friends and fans truly means that there is nothing that can stop me!

# The 7 P's for Success

**Purpose** - The next big breakthrough and period of growth came when I embraced a vision centered around helping others live healthier and better lives. When I took the focus off what I wanted, as far as growth and goals, and turned it toward how I could serve others, many doors started opening. Various mentors and the work of Simon Sinek influenced me. When we lead with our "Why" rather than the "How" and the "What," we connect with our audience on an emotional level, fostering loyalty and commitment. I embraced an idea articulated by the CEO of the company I partnered with: what we had to offer people was a gift of better health and a better way of life.

**Passion** - Your purpose will fuel your passion for what you do. It's critical that you have an unwavering belief that you have something of value to offer people. Your passion brings you the energy that attracts people and fuels your ability to continue through difficult moments.

**Persistence** - I've realized that persistence is not just a characteristic but a formidable ally in the pursuit of success. Everyone in business who is successful has experienced moments when they wanted to give up. When nothing is going right, you doubt your ability, and your vision gets cloudy. Persistence is what fuels your ability to take the next right action in the face of challenges and setbacks. I often come back to the wise words I heard in a workshop years ago.

"Doubt will take you out of action, and action will take you out of doubt."

This is what propels me forward when doubt creeps into my thinking even today. Once you let doubt take hold, you spiral down into fear, anxiety, and inactivity. Taking one small action of making a call, following up with a potential or current client, or making that social media post will break the cycle of doubt and renew your energy and enthusiasm.

Persistence gives me the determination to find a polite and inviting way to keep following up with potential and inactive clients. Sometimes it takes a day for someone to say "yes" to what you are offering, and sometimes it takes years!

Embracing persistence goes beyond weathering storms; it involves utilizing setbacks as stepping stones for personal and professional growth.

**Process** - To be effective and efficient in business, it is critical to have processes in place for acquiring new clients, keeping them coming back for more of your product or service, and training new employees and team members.

**Plan** - Whether it is a marketing plan, an in-person or online event or workshop, or a speech you will deliver, it is essential to develop this skill set of planning to become an Unstoppable Woman in business. Having the ability to break things down into steps and to see them coming to fruition before they happen is key.

**Practice** - The next step is to practice! Get a good mentor and practice telling your story, inviting, presenting, and following up. When we are developing new skill sets, there is a certain level of resistance. Our brain is telling us it is new and uncomfortable. By practicing, the resistance starts to fade. When you start, you will be bad. Sometimes embarrassingly bad. Keep at it. You will get better.

**Power** - Ultimately, your power and strength will come through the painful disappointments that are inevitable on your Unstoppable Woman journey. When we fully embrace the painful moments in life and business, we come to realize that these things happen for us, not to us. We find our strength in the pain. We find our true selves.

## Rewards of Entrepreneurship

One of the ways this entrepreneurial life has enriched me is that the skills I have developed and the person I have become have spilled over into my personal life and brought experiences and rewards that are priceless. One of the essential characteristics of a successful entrepreneur is to be a catalyst. Someone who starts things. Someone who gives birth to new ideas and experiences.

Every year for the past five years, I've set a new personal goal in my Living Younger Longer lifestyle. Turning 65 in 2023 merited something out of the ordinary. Early in the year, a desire that had been on the back burner for 30 years resurfaced. I wanted to hike the Grand Canyon again! From the moment I stepped back onto the South Rim with my husband at the end of my first "tour" of the Canyon, the idea of doing it again took root in my heart. This time around, I wanted to do it with a group of women, but I had no idea how I was going to find women who trusted me enough and had the desire to go on this adventure.

I still remember receiving my first definitive "Yes, I'm in," from a woman I had only met once before! That's when the Grand Canyon hike transformed from a wild idea into an adventure that was actually going to happen. My excitement went through the roof because I knew that my inviting skills had captured my first fellow hiker, and I was confident I would find more.

Although I was 30 years older, I entered into this project with less fear than I had the first time! Besides being in better physical shape and more knowledgeable about how to train for an endeavor like this, I had my business skill set to draw on for planning, preparing, and persisting through the inevitable tough spots.

The reality is that people die every year attempting to hike in the Grand Canyon. I took the planning and preparation part of the journey very seriously, from creating an itinerary that fit with the fitness and skill level of our group to making sure everyone had the gear they needed and had done the training necessary for a safe trip. My primary character trait of being persistent helped me keep the vision even when many of the women who initially said yes backed out.

In the end, our Fabulous Four group of intrepid hikers had a memorable and empowering experience. Although fulfilling my dream to hike the Canyon again was rewarding, the best part was sharing the experience with three women who had never backpacked before and instilling in them the desire to make backpacking a part of their life rather than a one-time adventure. From this accomplishment came a renewed trust in my power to be that catalyst, to achieve what I set out to do, and to bring value to the lives of people I know. Two of the most meaningful moments of this trip were the evening after we finished our hike when Jenna, who had done the hike with her mom Sandy, thanked me for all the work I put into the trip and for opening the door for her to experience this with her mom. And the second came a few months later when Sandy asked, "Where are we going next year?" These are priceless moments that I will cherish forever.

## Circle of Influence

One of the many blessings of this entrepreneurial life is that my circle of influence is so much larger than it ever would have been if I had stayed in the corporate world. Being an entrepreneur has opened the door for me to positively impact more lives.

Many of my friends became my clients, but my clients often become my dear friends as well. My business and personal life are woven together in this wonderful tapestry that enriches my life.

Although the entrepreneurial life required me to grow as a person and develop new skills, I recently realized that one of the foundational elements in my success is the creativity that was the hallmark of my career in the graphic arts industry. Through my experience as an author and speaker this past year, I am incorporating my life experiences dealing with co-dependency, mental illness, and addiction to serve a wider audience.

Over the last 15+ years, my purpose and vision for who I want to be and how I want to live my life and run my business have evolved into my motto, "Be More, Make More, Give More."

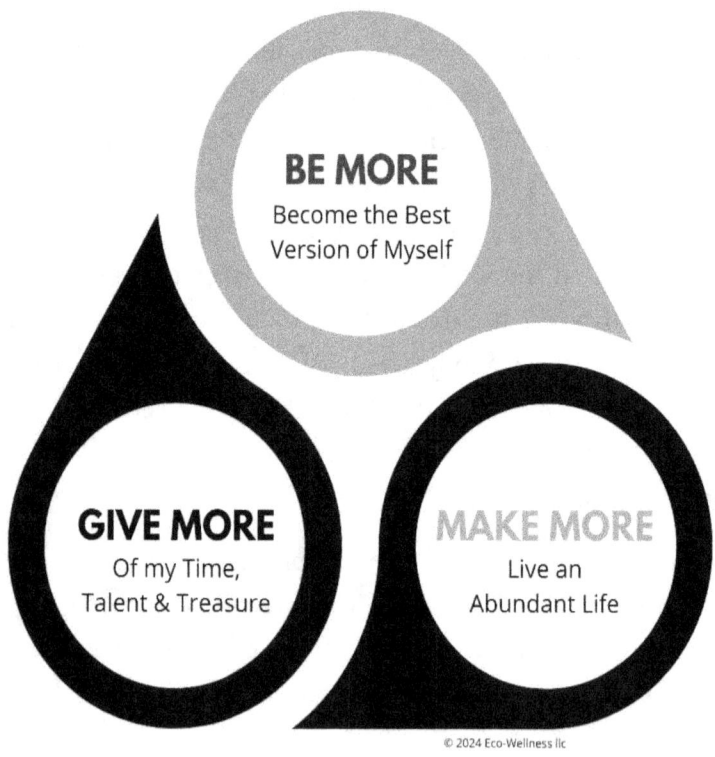

**BE MORE**
Become the Best
Version of Myself

**GIVE MORE**
Of my Time,
Talent & Treasure

**MAKE MORE**
Live an
Abundant Life

© 2024 Eco-Wellness llc

**Be More** - Becoming the best version of myself is a cycle of continual self-improvement. The goal is to fully develop the talents and opportunities God has given me so I can be of service to others.

**Make More** - This abundant life includes increasing my income, connections, and impact.

**Give More** - This is the ultimate goal. To become an extravagant giver of my time, talent, and treasure.

It's a never-ending cycle, with each segment leading into the next.

This is my formula for being an Unstoppable Woman!

I hope you have found some wisdom that you can weave into your own success story. My mission is to inspire you to become your healthiest self so you can best serve God and others. Whatever you want to achieve, I'll leave you with the theme and title of the first book I co-authored: "You Can, You Will."

**Sarena Diamond**

Founder and CEO of Diamond Solutions Group, LLC

https://www.linkedin.com/in/sarena-diamond/
https://www.facebook.com/sarena.diamond9/
https://www.instagram.com/sarenadiamond
https://diamondsolutionsgroupllc.com

Sarena Diamond is a transformation executive with deep expertise in Organizational Change Management, Leadership Development, Communications and Public Speaking. She is known for building high-performing teams while delivering challenging technology innovation, operational excellence, and process improvement initiatives.

As CEO and Founder of Diamond Solutions Group, LLC Sarena leverages experiences from Accenture, IBM, Pepsi Cola, and others to inspire outstanding outcomes for her clients. She is the master of the Power of **AND,** delivering impactful change and bringing leaders' visions to life in client environments ranging from Fortune 100 enterprises to PE-backed ventures.

Sarena holds an MBA from Pace University, a BS in Computer Science from Russell Sage College, and a certification in Collaborative

Storytelling for Social Impact from Georgetown University. She is an energetic public speaker, avid community volunteer, and conscientious board member. Most significantly, Sarena is "Mom" to three terrific adult kids and "Honey" to a loving, supportive partner.

# THE POWER OF AND

By Sarena Diamond

## Before And, There Was Only Or

Growing up, my sisters and I knew to keep quiet when Mom answered the phone with her "client voice". Having parents and grandparents who owned their own businesses, you learned different things than if your parents went to an office all day. Even as very little girls we could load Dad's restaurant Hobart dishwasher as efficiently as any busboy, provided there was a 5-gallon bucket nearby to boost us up high enough to reach. One might say that I am genetically predisposed to be an entrepreneur and as much as "children learn what they live", the entrepreneurial lessons that would eventually inspire me to follow in my family's footsteps were definitely slow to materialize. Before that could happen, I would need to learn the most powerful three-letter word in the alphabet… AND.

Throughout my childhood and teen years, I saw my parents work and work and work… long hours, difficult customers, no time off, and family vacations were completely foreign. By comparison, my friends' parents relaxed on weekends, hosted fancy-looking dinner parties with "people from the office", and went on summer vacations every year. Perhaps, like most teenagers, the grass definitely looked greener on the other side. I was determined to make my way in the world differently than my entrepreneurial role models. I set my sights on a "glamorous corporate career", and luckily, my mom encouraged my dreams even if she didn't really understand them.

I knew my plans would require a college degree. I also knew college would cost money that my family simply didn't have. Successful entrepreneurs instill industrious DNA in their kids, and New Hampshire authorizes working papers at fourteen with parental permission. I had already been babysitting every day after school, on weekends, and during summers for two years by my fourteenth birthday and had quite a bit saved for college. With working papers in hand, jobs as a waitress, scooping ice cream, and cooking short-order breakfasts increased the contributions to my college savings account. All those jobs reinforced childhood lessons about working hard, being reliable, and doing a job well, but did little else to prepare me to fit into my post-college corporate endeavors.

I graduated magna cum laude with a BS degree in Computer Science and Management from an unlikely liberal arts college in upstate New York. Landing in the world of a "Big-6" consulting company after graduation was as far away from entrepreneurial as I could have gotten. I loved every bit of the challenge, the pace, and the professionalism that my newfound corporate career at Accenture provided. Performance reviews reinforced that my capabilities were aligned with my goals and then some. I was proud of the work I was doing and how I was making my long-held dreams come true.

Over the next 17 years, I moved on from Accenture to other Fortune 100 company roles at PepsiCola, Hyperion, and Melon, each with bigger titles, greater responsibilities, and larger teams to lead. Along the way, Pepsi sponsored my Executive MBA studies, furthering my professional development and building my confidence in my skills. I was proud of the level of business impact I was making and confident that I was worthy of my big corner office and generous executive compensation package.

During those years, my young family also flourished. My college sweetheart and I were married with three beautiful children, a big house in the suburbs of New York City, and a comfortable distance from the financial stresses of my childhood. Little did I know that a highly unremarkable, blonde cliché would come along and torch my idyllic life. My self-confidence was cratered at the same time the financial aftermath of 9/11 and the Enron scandal wreaked havoc on my industry and my career. That betrayal would be my first, but not last, gut-wrenching lesson to redefine my world.

Spending days on end crying in my bed was not an option I could afford for long, at least not with a divorce attorney, household bills, and school-aged children to support. Reaching out and reconnecting with MBA colleagues led me to a job at IBM that was stable, interesting enough, and provided most of the financial resources we needed… even if it was more than a few rungs lower on that corporate ladder. My priority was my children's well-being, and for the next 18 years, it was the absolute right decision for all four of us. I worked a lot but traveled very little, supported their schooling, shuttled them to sports, and coached their extracurriculars. I jumped into education-related volunteerism and board service to further challenge my mind but kept my schedule open for my kids' activities and our nightly family dinners. Colleagues who knew me before IBM often asked if I regretted making such drastic changes. Honestly, while I missed the prior financial freedom, I truly did not regret a moment of the added time with my children. The only regrets would come less than a year after leaving IBM when a second hard-learned lesson in betrayal left me questioning my own judgment and doubting I would ever trust a corporate leader again.

Ten days before Christmas my six-month position as Partner of Organizational Change Management at a large international corporation was eliminated without warning or indication. The boss who had lured me to the role with an equal blend of compelling vision and charismatic flattery delivered the news over a video chat that lasted less than two minutes. The terms of my severance package were strict and silencing. The trauma of that action was palpable, despite receiving a year of professional outplacement services and a hefty severance package that they hoped would entice me to forgive and forget. The reality of suddenly being "in transition" in my mid-fifties had a gravity to it that I should have given much more appreciation. Instead, I went to Hawaii.

We had a family vacation planned long in advance and while it might have been financially prudent to have canceled, I truly NEEDED this trip. My soul was renewed with each stunning sunrise over Oahu and the breathtaking sunset from the top of Mauna Kea. Those warm sun rays were like an encouraging hug from my heavenly family members. Somewhere on that tropical vacation, the idea of "going out on my own" was sparked.

I quickly learned that it is not at all easy to transition from corporate life filled with team members, common infrastructure, and technology like email and calendars. Where reusable templates and marketing collateral are readily available and maintained by graphic design experts. Where there are a whole host of resources and people available to answer questions, collaborate on challenges and help solve them, and provide validation or at least constructive feedback on your own ideas. After 30+ years in corporate America, I had a lot of foundational building blocks to establish as an entrepreneur without the time or patience to do so.

I knew I needed a network, as I had been less than consistent in maintaining my corporate connections outside of IBM. When times were extremely busy, I had often neglected those relationship-building activities. Building a business required diverse and deeply trusted relationships and I had to start over from scratch.

I made LinkedIn my daily obsession, connecting with long-lost colleagues and directly messaging all of my holiday card list of friends. Announcing my new venture became easier when accompanied by the question I had learned in one of the many solopreneur education programs: "Who do you know that needs my help?" The overwhelming good wishes and encouragement bolstered my spirits but didn't help me get any closer to landing a gig. Little did I know my mindset and approach were stuck in old, corporate ways, and I needed to get back to my entrepreneurial roots if I was going to succeed.

I accepted an invitation to join Chief, the relatively new network of C-suite female executives, and spent an uncomfortable amount of my severance check on the cost of annual membership. That investment would pay back tenfold when I landed an engagement opportunity from within the network, but that wouldn't happen for months.

## The Power of And

Audrey Martin was a stranger until she became a friend and one of my biggest supporters. I had been studying the new rules of job hunting for weeks, networking with thinly-veiled confidence, and applying for countless opportunities with little success and growing apprehension. A job search contact heard my background and aspirations and encouraged me to reach out to Audrey, who was an experienced consultant and executive coach. We had similar corporate backgrounds and spoke the same language. The connection was immediate and even though all I could offer the relationship were insecure experiential woes, Audrey validated my half-baked musings and bolstered my confidence. She would soon ask me the question that turned my world around.

Often, Audrey and I connected to compare opportunities we were seeing, share connections, and strategize on service offerings. I was struggling to find a unique value proposition. I had countless different possible avenues I could pursue, and I was not convinced that it would not be better to go back to a "corporate job" even though I knew I would never be truly happy or trusting. Still, I would find a promising job posting, get my hopes up, and research everything I could about this one single company or opportunity, simply in hopes of being viewed favorably if I got the opportunity to interview or pitch. Each day, the depressing cycle would repeat.

In the middle of sharing these challenges, Audrey interrupted and asked simply, "Why do you keep saying 'or'? What about 'and'?" As she explained her question and reminded me of the wealth of experience I had accumulated throughout my career, for the first time I considered that maybe my future path was not linear, but instead intended to be multi-directional. There were a wide variety of opportunities to be experienced in any way, shape, or form, all of which might bring me joy. In those nine simple words, Audrey demonstrated brilliance and wisdom that changed my trajectory as I launched onto the "And" path.

Within 24 hours, I registered my newly minted business name, Diamond Solutions Group, LLC with an articulated goal to "establish a pipeline of consulting work comparable to next year's corporate earnings before severance ends".

AND

Within 48 hours, I connected with 17 C-suite leaders on LinkedIn, asking direct and leading questions about changes happening in their organization.

AND

Within 96 hours, I pitched 14 engagement proposals through two talent-sourcing agencies and had five interviews for consultant roles.

Clearly, there was power in that three-letter word, AND. As soon as I decided that I could do any number of different things, not simply focusing on the single, linear opportunity in front of me, my entrepreneurial acceleration began. My approach to landing an engagement became "multi-faceted". Daily reach-outs to direct connections. Countless check-ins across my network. Collaborative conversations with as many talent pool resource managers as would talk with me. My success rate with client interviews rose with my confidence level. When asked a question about my experiences and what kind of companies I worked for, I coined a response on the fly that surprised even me, saying, "Well, actually, I don't work for companies. I work for people."

That response landed me my first Organizational Change engagement for an entertainment equipment rental and service company. The contract lasted 10 months, earned me premiere flight and hotel status, and enabled me to surpass my earnings goals by almost 175%. More importantly, this first client engagement established my unique value proposition and initiated a new trajectory for this third chapter of my career.

My appreciation for the talent companies doing the dreaded business development activity grew, as did my creativity in approaching potential business opportunities in an "anti-cold calling" way. Job posts for full-time executive roles became an opportunity to offer my services on a short-term basis while the full-time hire was found and on-boarded. Announcements of newly appointed leaders inspired me to offer congratulations to complete strangers and inquire about possible collaboration on challenges they might discover in their new jobs. My favorite was seeking out women who had experienced similar career traumas and brainstorming ways to help them put the pieces back together for their next chapter. I experienced real joy and tremendous personal benefits with all these unique approaches to "business development" and made some amazing connections, in addition to good karma, along the way. I grew to learn that when an entrepreneur truly, selflessly supports another entrepreneur, just as Audrey had done with me, magic happens!

"The Power of And" continued to be my success criteria. Whenever I was faced with a difficult either/or choice, I searched for the "And" in the situation. An engagement focused on delivering sales training grew into an opportunity to mentor young executives. Creating a communications strategy expanded into professional speaking and hosting a workshop of 350 organizational leaders on "*Delivering on Objectives And Demonstrating Core Values in Leadership*". Client appreciation for my delivering the "And" they needed came in the form of contract extensions and professional referrals.

As the end of the first year of Diamond Solutions Group, LLC approached, I was presented with a difficult test of my commitment to my entrepreneur status. A significant client engagement was reaching conclusion, so I was not surprised to be invited to a meeting with the executive leader. I left that meeting mulling over a generous offer to join their company as a full-time executive, working with people I enjoyed, in an industry that was both exciting and fun. Tempting as it was to consider resuming the bi-weekly W-2 paycheck stability, comforting health benefits, and lucrative bonuses, the decision was easier when I realized I would have to shelve my consulting work, or severely limit what I could do for clients in an after-hours capacity. There would be no "And".

This would not be the last time my commitment to being an entrepreneur would be tested, yet to date, the decision to remain has always proved to be the right one for me. As my parents and grandparents had experienced, being a solopreneur has meant lots of long hours, client travel away from my family, and some fear of financial uncertainty as consulting engagements ended without knowing the next move. Yet, the freedom to choose who I work for and truly enjoy working with the clients I help has bolstered my enthusiasm for being on my own. Knowing that there is no shortage of opportunities to apply the experiences and expertise gained during my corporate career fills me with optimism for the future of my company. Encouraging other entrepreneurs to find the path to joy for themselves reinforces that decision to keep going and gives me an appreciation for my ancestors who chose to do the same each and every day of their lives. "The Power of And" is the epitome of being successful as an entrepreneur, especially when the "And" you empower is your belief in yourself.

## Nita McKinley

CEO of Firehouse Deliveries LLC

https://www.facebook.com/nita.mckinley.39
https://www.instagram.com/nitamckinley09
https://www.thefirehousedeliveries.com/

Nita McKinley, a single mother from Los Angeles, California, has endured unimaginable loss, with her son tragically murdered three years ago. Amidst this grief, she shoulders the responsibility of raising her grandchildren without their father. Despite the pain, reminders of her son persist, as her grandchildren call his phone, longing for connection.

Transitioning to a new chapter of her life, Nita faces a cascade of challenges. Forced to leave her home of twenty-three years, she finds herself homeless, moving from hotel to hotel. Compounding her struggles, she navigates complex legal battles as a trustee for her deceased family members, grappling with issues ranging from stolen property to greedy heirs.

Despite these hardships, Nita's resilience shines through. At age 65, she ventured into the cannabis industry, guided by a divine opportunity rather than age-based stereotypes. Reflecting on her corporate career, she recalls years of feeling trapped, undervalued, and overlooked.

Eventually, she was fired, liberating her from the confines of corporate life and prompting a newfound sense of freedom.

Embracing uncertainty, Nita embarked on her entrepreneurial journey. Encountering the Social Equity Program—an initiative aimed at rectifying injustices in communities disproportionately impacted by marijuana laws—Nita unexpectedly found herself drawn into the cannabis business. Despite initial reluctance, she applied and ultimately secured licensing, navigating bureaucratic hurdles and financial strains along the way.

Her journey is marked by sacrifice and resilience. Nita poured her resources, including equity from her home, into her business, weathering financial turmoil and foreclosure threats. Despite the challenges, she remains steadfast, striving for success in an industry fraught with complexities.

As Nita awaits approval for a storefront retail license, she acknowledges the mistakes and challenges ahead. Yet, she remains undeterred, proud to be her own boss, and determined to overcome any obstacles that lie ahead.

# STARTING A CANNABIS BUSINESS AT 65

By Nita McKinley

Hi, my name is Nita McKinley. I am a single mother living in Los Angeles, California. I am growing through adverse experiences. My son was killed right in front of my home three years ago. All four people who helped murder my son are in jail except one out on probation. They said it was a drive-by. Then they said mistaken identity, but I will never know. All I know is that my son is gone, and I am left with four children, my grandchildren, without their father. They still try to contact him by calling his phone to let him know what is going on in their lives even though they know he's passed. Some still have nightmares.

How did I get here? This is a new chapter in my life. As I write this chapter of my life, I'm packing and moving out of my house after twenty-three years. I'm homeless with no plan B on my agenda. Hotel to Hotel until the money runs out. My computer was dropped by someone without telling me. Now I have to get it fixed. I'm in the middle of court cases. I am a trustee for my mother, aunt, and cousin who passed away in 2014, 2017, and 2018 respectively. My mom is a victim of her home being stolen, my aunt has tax issues, and my cousin has greedy children. I'm being sued by one of the criminals in my mom's case for not taking them off the judgment that my mom won against all of the criminals involved. Yes, how did I get here?

I started a cannabis business at age 65. Someone once asked me, "What made you go into a millennial business?"

I said, "Wow, I didn't know it was a millennial business; all I know is God opened the door and I walked in." I'm quite sure if the door had sung their way they would have walked in too.

I worked in the corporate world for thirty years. I was so trapped, thinking I was living the life because of who I worked for. It all sounded so important. I had a good job and made a lot of money, well, at least I thought I did. I was living paycheck to paycheck. I worked hard with endless hours but never got rewarded. I just wanted to go to work, do my job, and live peacefully with a loving life. Instead, I was unhealthy, unhappy, and depressed. I held a significant position in many people's lives, and throughout the ups and downs and the most challenging times, I would keep a happy and smiling face. I would surround myself with positivity, brightness, and love even when I wasn't feeling well.

I'm a fighter. I have been a fighter all my life. I never give up without trying. I have always faced trials and tribulations with a smile. "I know trouble doesn't always last and joy will come." I always try to see the good in everything and everybody. I believe in karma. I believe if I crossed your path, it's for a reason and just for a season. I'm a limited edition. I'm a diamond and not just a jewel. I played the game for thirty years trying to climb the ladder of success, but instead, I endured jealousy, envy, hate, and racism. My second language played a deep part in it all just because I knew the language and had a degree in it. I loved being a service to the public but management can be cruel and abuse their authoritative power.

I was always told, "Go to school get a good job and work for someone else." I prayed and asked God to take me out of the corporate world. I was fired three weeks after that prayer. My mom always said, "The things that proceed out of your mouth are the things you hope for." I saw the writing on the wall. I was going to get pushed out because of my age or just plainly fired. When I got fired, I felt I didn't want to work for anyone else anymore. I was one of those employees who "stuck and stayed" in the same position but not by choice. I spent my forties, fifties, and sixties trapped not being able to go anywhere else. I thought I didn't have a choice to go anywhere else. I was trapped in making what I thought was a lot of money. I was going to be promoted to a higher level. I endured the madness every day for thirty years. Getting fired was the best thing that could have happened to me. I no longer have to work for people who don't like me and won't promote me. I wasn't promoted not because I wasn't good at what I did but because I wasn't liked. My life was trapped in a corporate mindset. Corporate had me. I was scared to move on to an uncertain world, not being able to live from paycheck to paycheck as I had thus far. I had a lifestyle to maintain and responsibilities to pay bills. I was the scared one, trapped in working for the corporate world, living from paycheck to paycheck. At first, I had to take into consideration I had no security; I lost a regular paycheck, fringe benefits, vacation pay, retirement, and a 401k program. If you don't plan it right, you will receive only $400 a month like me from corporate.

I now live life without entrapment. I am now sickness free. I am not in and out of the hospital anymore. I'm enjoying life and I travel when I want to without asking. You can take back your life at any age. It's an old saying, "You're only as old as you feel." I don't feel old. Age doesn't matter, but we do. I'm elderly but not old. Dreamers become owners and bosses; it's never too late, even at age sixty-five. I worked hard, and now I finally got my promotion. I am the owner and boss of my own company. I still hold a significant position in many people's lives. People depend on my services medically to help with their pain and recreationally to have fun and enjoy the moment.

## Jacqueline Long

Elevate Your Biz Coaching & Consulting
CEO, Business Marketing Strategist,
Master Certified Mindset Coach

https://www.facebook.com/profile.php?id=100084595752055
https://instagram.com/elevateyourbizcoachingllc
https://www.facebook.com/JacquelineLongElevateYourBizOfficialPage

Jacqueline is a Business Marketing Strategist, Podcast Host, Master Certified Transformation & Mindset Coach.

She helps women start & scale coaching businesses online. She is the Founder of Elevate Your Biz Coaching and Consulting, LLC - her official brand dedicated to women upleveling in life & business.

Jacqueline holds three graduate degrees (a Master of Public Administration, MS in Human Resources Management & MA in Criminal Justice). Prior to starting her coaching business, she had a 22-yr career in social services. She has served as a Director of Case Management, Director of Social Services, Director of AIDS Clinical Trials and Vice President of Human Resources.

Jacqueline is a native New Yorker. Her family is originally from the

Caribbean islands of Trinidad and Tobago. She enjoys music, traveling, reading, and studying languages. She has two daughters and lives in the Atlanta, Metro area. Currently, Jacqueline working on her PhD in Education.

# THE GIFT

## By Jacqueline Long

*"What you tell yourself about yourself, about your life, about your limitations, you will believe."*
– Iyanla Vanzant

I don't often share my personal story. I have never found it to be especially inspiring, and being vulnerable doesn't come naturally to me. You see, I grew up tough. I am the youngest of 14 children who grew up in the East Flatbush section of Brooklyn, New York. I was the "baby" and the last child at home, raised by my mom and a great stepfather who didn't live in my home. I come from a traditional Caribbean family of mixed African, Asian, and European ancestry from the beautiful twin islands of Trinidad & Tobago. The odds were against me growing up. The neighborhood I grew up in predicted I would become a statistic, fall to the streets, drugs, teenage pregnancy, jail, or worse.

As a child, however, I was smart beyond my years, and very curious, with a thirst for knowledge. I did well in school and graduated valedictorian of my high school class. I went on to graduate from college and complete three graduate degrees. In the mid-90s, I started my career in the nonprofit sector working with the HIV/AIDS population. I started as an HIV testing counselor and worked my way up to Director of Social Services and then Vice President of Human Resources. After 20+ years in my profession, I moved to Atlanta, Georgia and decided to do something new. I left my profession and started my own business and podcast and became a co-author for the first time. Today, I manage my own business, and I'm working on my Ph.D. in Education. Along the way, I managed to raise two beautiful daughters, a 23-year-old college graduate and grad student, and a 20-year-old soon-to-be college graduate. Now in my early fifties, while I still have many dreams and desires to pursue, I look back at how far I've come and think to myself, "How in the world did I do it all?" I'll admit, I am a bit of an overachiever. But I'm not exceptionally talented or gifted, by any means.

## LIFE LESSONS

I had very little growing up. However, I was surrounded by family and family friends who served as positive role models in my life. I learned at a young age that there was life beyond my environment. There was no demand for me to go to college. But no matter what I wanted to do with my life, my mother supported me. She was my biggest cheerleader. It would take me years to realize that my drive, motivation, and fearlessness to try new things and accomplish my goals, came from her.

My mother didn't have much. However, what she gave me was invaluable. These were "gifts" she passed on that would play a profound role in who I would become. These gifts were gratitude and a positive mindset. My mother believed that with gratitude, prayer, and positive thoughts, you could attract whatever you wanted in your life. While I would learn more about manifesting, later in life, she taught me very early how to manifest or attract what I wanted with the power of my own thinking. Whenever I had doubts about something, my mother would say, "You WILL get through.", or "Light a candle, pray, and do something that makes you feel good. Tell yourself, "You WILL make it happen and it must happen for you. It's God's will." Her words were always comforting. They gave me the power and drive I needed to go after my dreams.

My mom passed away in January 2020. She was my greatest gift. And her memories, words, and lessons will stay with me forever. She was a wise and strong woman. She prayed and was always grateful for what we had. I always found it eerie that she would say something out loud and later it would come to fruition. She never complained and always told me to think and believe! She taught me that one of the keys to success in life is establishing a positive mindset to acquire and attract whatever I want. My mother's positive thinking would truly prove to be a gift in my life.

## ONLY IF YOU BELIEVE

Ironically, while my mom had mastered the power of manifesting, she didn't use it to pursue any of her dreams. She often used her positive thinking to just get by. Mom was able to manifest powerfully, but she was from a different generation and she struggled with what many of us struggle with, limiting beliefs, or the negative or limiting thoughts that we have around what we can achieve or have in life. As a woman, a professional, and an entrepreneur, my mom's lessons have shown me that you can only achieve what you believe you can. And whatever you think, is what will actually be. What you limit yourself to is what you will have. Therefore, belief and establishing a positive mindset are significant parts of achieving success. I've learned that there is no limit to what we can achieve or have, unless we place limits on ourselves, through our own thinking. Achieving an unlimited mindset happens through practicing positive thinking, and working on self-development, spirituality, and self-care consistently.

We are complex human beings, and we must have clarity on our goals and fill our cups, nourish ourselves physically, mentally, emotionally, and spiritually, to achieve success. I am not a religious guru or even an expert in spirituality or self-care. However, there was a time in my life when I felt stuck, bored, and disillusioned with life. I knew there was more that I wanted to do. But I had hit a limit in my thinking, where I didn't believe I could achieve anything more than I already had. I struggled for a while. And once again, my mother's wisdom would help me to move forward. She told me to get clear on what I wanted, pray, be grateful and take action. And so, I did.

## YOU CAN'T POUR FROM A EMPTY CUP

In my forties, I would go on to start my own business and achieve many of the goals that I set for myself. I built on the foundation that I learned from my mom- to get clear and think positively in pursuit of my goals. I mastered the art of manifesting and taking action. I now pay close attention to my thoughts and words, and avoid negative energy. I nurture my mind with things that challenge my thinking, and I learn about wealth consciousness and spirituality. In other words, I make strengthening my mindset a DAILY habit. This has become non-negotiable for me. The more inner work, development of the mind, and self-care work we practice, the better we're able to attract our desires, and cope with doubt and stress in uncertain times. One of the mottos that I am learning to live by is, "You can't pour from an empty cup." As cliché as it may sound, it's the absolute truth in life. You simply cannot give of yourself what you do not have. And unfortunately, through my own experience and working with women in my professional and business career, I have found that women have the "pour from an empty cup syndrome." We take care of everyone else's needs, yet we neglect our own. I truly believe that my mom may have suffered from this, as well. She was so busy trying to provide and keep her head above water that she had no time to think or manifest her own goals and desires. I know that I too have experienced the same while working full-time, pursuing my education, and caring for my family. I ran myself ragged. I lost touch with my desires and goals, abandoned self-care and became bored and disinterested in my goals.

## IT STARTS WITH YOU

Today, I remind myself and others that there is a reason we are reminded to place our oxygen masks on first when we board a flight. Developing your mindset, self-love and self-care are about making sure YOU can breathe first, so that you can help OTHERS around you to breathe as well. Success and having what you desire starts with YOU. It's about taking care of yourself, so that you can achieve what you desire, to better support the ones you love. It's about thinking positively, setting your goals, staying in a high vibe, and knowing there are no limits to what you can have or achieve. If you can think it, you can have it. When I share this, I'm often asked about my own mindset practices, and what I do to maintain a positive mindset and manage my own limiting beliefs. I believe they think that the daily practices that have helped me to achieve my own dreams and successes, are special. But the truth is, they are not. Achieving my desires and goals starts with what my mom originally taught me, establishing clarity on what I want, believing I can have it and being grateful for what I already have. My daily practice includes some additional practices that work for me. But I keep them very simple. If you want to focus more on achieving your goals, identifying your own GIFTS, and having what you want in life, the ONE thing you need to know is it starts with YOU and the way you THINK. I'm sharing some of the daily practices that I enjoy and are helpful to me, in the next section.

## MY STRATEGIES FOR MINDSET AND SUCCESS

Here are some recommendations for working on your own mindset daily, to achieve more of what you desire. These are some of the strategies that I use in my daily routine to work on my mindset, self-care and to support achieving my goals. I do some of these practices daily and others occasionally. I also switch them up from time to time. I invite you to use any of the strategies that may be helpful to you:

**Gratitude–** I practice gratitude daily. As I wake, I write 3-5 things or MORE that I am grateful for in my life. I'm a strong believer in being grateful for what I have, before creating and acquiring more. I also remind myself to say "thank you" to God/the universe and people, throughout the day, as often as I can.

I live by this personal mantra: Gratitude = (a better) Attitude = (an elevated) Altitude, in life.

**Journaling**– If you had asked me about journaling several years ago, I would have said NEVER would I put my thoughts on paper. However, one of my coaches turned me on to this with a 21-day challenge and I've never looked back. Journaling helps me to think. It's a great way to gain clarity, dump what's going on internally, and ask for divine guidance or inspired action when needed. I enjoy journaling daily. I use this to both clear my mind and explore options or "downloads"/guidance for things that I'm confused about or need to work out. I also journal about the things I'm grateful for and I'm manifesting at any given time. Journaling is one of my favorite things to do for myself. You'd be surprised how the answers to things you're struggling with, will come to you, after writing them down on paper.

**Prayer**– As I mentioned previously, I am spiritual, not religious. Prayer is important to me. My belief in a higher power is a significant part of my life. And my spiritual beliefs are an important part of everything I do.

**Reading**– I read for self-development and/or personal entertainment, daily. It helps me to learn new things, nurture my growth process, relax, laugh, and sometimes escape the daily grind (especially now).

**Affirmations/Mantras**– I use my mantras (I have several) and create more as needed. I use them to reinforce my NEW beliefs around things that I struggle with. In other words, I identify limiting beliefs that I may have around growth, wealth, or self-care, and I create new beliefs and say them out loud, daily to reprogram my mind with the NEW beliefs.

**High Vibe Playlist**– I LOVE music. Music will truly pick me up whenever I'm in a funk. I've created a "high-vibe" playlist of music that always puts me in a good mood. This is especially helpful to me when

I am feeling down or manifesting something I desire. When you feel good, you attract good. Therefore, staying in a high vibe is a MUST.

**Quiet Time–** This is essential for me. I carve out 60- minutes daily (sometimes longer), for MYSELF. I let everyone in the house know that I am having quiet time and I do NOT want to be disturbed. I have very strict boundaries around this time. I use this time for a little meditation, reading, listening to music, or doing anything that feels good and nurtures my spirit. Sometimes I take a nap. However, this is NOT the time that I do mindset practice. I do mindset work in the morning. This is just ME time, to quiet myself and connect with myself and feel good. This is the time that I usually get the MOST and BEST inspiration for new ideas or the solution to a problem.

**Meditation–** This one is NEW for me and not always the same as quiet time. Meditation is a little more focused. I'm learning to quiet my mind from the external noise of life in business and at home, raising a family. I have to be honest; I've found meditation challenging because quieting the mind is NOT an easy thing. It requires complete focus - but focus on- NOTHING. That is incredibly difficult for me. My mind is constantly in overdrive. That's exactly why I realized that I very much need to practice sitting still with my thoughts. It's a powerful strategy for quieting the mind, caring for your inner being, and gaining inspiration.

**Walking–** A little daily exercise is good for us physically, emotionally, and mentally. I am generally terrible at exercising. But, I'm slowly getting better at incorporating more exercise into my daily routine for overall good health and wellness. I love walking, inside on the treadmill, and outside in nature. It helps me to think and clear my thoughts while raising my heart rate a little. There's something about connecting with nature on a sunny day that can put me in the most high-vibe and loving spirits.

Finally, these strategies are just a few of the practices that support my mind, foster my growth, and help me take care of myself. I continue to add strategies for self-care and mindset. I have created my own little high-vibe, mindset toolkit that I can tap into as a resource to stay focused, positive, and cope with stress and doubt when they set in. As you can see, what I do daily is NOTHING fancy. However, these are the things that help me to feel good, think, achieve my goals, and take better care of myself and my family. When I am not nurturing myself, I can't run a successful business or support my loved ones. It starts with ME. If I want more for them, then I must give myself the gift of doing MORE for MYSELF. I want more women to learn this and put it into practice. A successful and elevated life is NOT just about hard work and getting everything done; it's also about believing in yourself, thinking positively, taking care of yourself, setting goals and nurturing your growth, so that you can achieve and have more of what you desire and deserve.

Elevate!

## Joan Soto Melendez

Rumbo Al Bienestar, LLC
CEO and License Professional Counselor

https://www.linkedin.com/in/joansoto/en
https://www.facebook.com/rumboalbienestarllc/
https://www.instagram.com/rumboalbienestarllc/
https://rumboalbienestarllc.com/

Joan Soto is a licensed professional counselor in Connecticut. Graduated from Central Connecticut University with a Master's degree in Clinical Professional Counseling. In addition, she has been a therapist for nearly 10 years. Ms. Soto is an entrepreneur and also a thriver. Especially because she faced domestic violence in the past. She is the CEO of Rumbo al Bienestar, LLC. Today, when she's not traveling, you'll often find her performing therapeutic sessions to provide emotional support, especially to Latinas that are healing from abusive relationships. My aspiration is to continue promoting mental health as a key to heal and how survivors could build a bright future. To learn more about Joan Soto and how she could help you in your recovery journey, visit: https://rumboalbienestarllc.com/.

# STEPS TO BECOME AN ENTREPRENEUR AFTER FACING ADVERSITY

By Joan Soto Melendez

## A Promising Young Woman with a Lack of Possibilities

Being an outstanding girl in primary school is not a promise of a bright future. The questions at the front of many people's minds could be: what are the components to succeed as an entrepreneur? Especially when you were not born in a golden crib with a rich family, what possibilities does a Latina female with a dream have? I used to imagine that I could create a better world. But my opportunities were scarce, especially because my parents did not go to college. I also remember that my father and grandmother used to be loyal to employment despite the challenges they faced. I even witnessed my grandmother being verbally attacked by one of her bosses. I did not want to have the same future that my past generation overcame.

In Puerto Rico, many young people do not find employment in the career they graduate from. And even more challenging is to find at least a decent job that offers a good salary. In PR the minimum wage is $9.50 per hour and this does not reflect the inflationary trends. To give an example, according to the US Department of Labor: The highest insured unemployment rate in the week ending June 27 2020 was in Puerto Rico (26.8) but in Connecticut was (15.2)[1]. I did not want to be part of those statistics. I used to think that being optimistic was not enough to create my successful path. As a result, my existential question

---

[1] Source:
https://www.dol.gov/sites/dolgov/files/eta/Performance/pdfs/annual_economic_reports/2021/PR%20Economic%20Analysis%20Report%20FY%202020-2021%20(00000002)%20en%20pdf.pdf

was how I can move forward toward my goals. I had a blurred flashback of a summit that I attended in South Africa in 2013 while I was typing the first draft of this chapter on my computer. One Young World was the name of the summit, and that was the first time I heard the word "entrepreneurship." To be honest, that blew my mind, and I remember that I started doing some research about it.

Looking back, many experiences shaped my entrepreneurial skill set. However, that was not enough to "break the glass ceiling". After I migrated from Puerto Rico around 10 years ago, I thought to myself, "Now that I am in the land of opportunity I will be able to triumph." I was not totally wrong in terms of becoming successful in the USA. The only inaccurate detail was related to the fantasy of the American dream without the ability to overcome invisible barriers, including discrimination, cultural challenges, biases and assumptions, etc. from different employers. As an Afro-Latina, some employers tried to discourage me from going into managerial positions. That is why I began to "cook a new recipe" to become an entrepreneur, even when no one believed I could do it.

## My Ingredients to Thrive

When I became an adult, I got married. I used to look for someone to love me without knowing how important it was to love the person that I always saw in the mirror... myself. Probably, the fact that I did not know as a young woman how to value myself, then the person who I chose to be my partner did not understand my worth. I faced domestic violence and I hit the ground. Thankfully, I was able to get happily divorced and was ready to start a new chapter of my life. However, there were some roots of bitterness, lack of self-confidence, and insecurities. Yes, I am a therapist, but also a survivor and a Latina single mother. That is why I wondered what the possibilities were for me. That is when I developed my new mantra or affirmation: when there is a struggle, there is a possibility to create the right set of circumstances. I started to bloom from my optimism. Therefore, the first ingredients I would like to bring to the Thrive recipe are faith and hope. Before applying those ingredients, I felt lost and hopeless. Then, I promised myself that this would be the beginning of a new chapter full of blessings. I understood that my sadness was a feeling about my past. I validated myself for three years. Honestly, it was a tough life transition. And currently, I could say that my life challenges were my university. I understood and embraced my transformation process through my spiritual journey.

The principal fact that I treasure with all my heart is what I found in the following statement in the Bible:

"Therefore, since we have been made right in God's sight by faith, we have peace with God because of what Jesus Christ our Lord has done for us. Because of our faith, Christ has brought us into this place of undeserved privilege where we now stand, and we confidently and joyfully look forward to sharing God's glory. We can rejoice, too, when we run into problems and trials, for we know that they help us develop endurance. And endurance develops strength of character, and character strengthens our confident hope of salvation. And this hope will not lead to disappointment. For we know how dearly God loves us because he has given us the Holy Spirit to fill our hearts with his love." (Romans 5:1-5 NLT) With that said, now I am aware that many of the adversities that I overcame built up my fruit of the spirits, including love, joy, peace, forbearance, kindness, goodness, faithfulness, gentleness, and self-control. At the moment when things appear to fall apart, it is normal to ask why it is happening to me. To master challenging situations, you need to allow God to take control of your battles. That is why my faith has been key to thriving.

My next ingredient was to increase my self-love and focus on finding my interests. I traveled, I failed and fell, and I got up. I started to fall in love with every one of my imperfections, my strengths, and my weaknesses. The search for my purpose to create my new meaning was fundamental. Before practicing self-love, I felt broken and I was in grief. However, I had to develop a new mindset. I start connecting with myself, prioritizing my needs, and creating a space full of peace and harmony. Moreover, another element has been refining my self-care techniques. For example, setting boundaries, exercise, food as medicine, going to my primary doctor regularly, etc. It is especially important to consider all the human components including physical and mental health, socialization, promoting healthy relationships, etc. I have learned that caring about me is a self-love act. There is no doubt that practicing self-love is a significant element in our entrepreneurial path. Making time for that likely seems to be impossible. For me, developing a structured life has been vital to keeping my mind balanced. My wellness plan is defined by God, myself, and my clinical team.

A further component is that I believe in myself and that I am a masterpiece in progress. I empower myself and continue to build up my resilience. And I have to add that the ingredient of resilience must be combined with the 5 D's: determination, discipline, dedication, developing a flexible cognition, and dropping old suitcases. The first three have been cited by many experts to be the key to success. I firmly believe that combining them with cognitive flexibility makes a great equation for entrepreneurship. Especially because a flexible mindset allows us to adjust to different tasks, roles, and responsibilities we are presented with each day. It is important to evaluate our frame of mind, including our perceptions, emotions, actions, and even our deep motivations. And at the same time, being open to think and act out of the box. Do not forget that a rigid mindset will keep you stuck in life. Also, you will need to unpack all the different stuff that does not belong in the present moment. It is valid to have difficult memories of our past experiences. However, it is not recommended to continue suffering from those events that you already dealt with. The last ingredient is non-stop dreaming and setting a deadline for your goals. Basically, having a goal without a deadline is just a dream. And dreaming is fine but that itself does not provide you with a plan to become an entrepreneur.

## Mental Health is the Key to Healing

Having a therapist in my life has been fundamental to my healing process. Additionally, these services help me to cultivate my emotional health and understand how important it is to fill my cup first. Also, it is key to understanding ways to cope with stress and developing awareness about my trauma responses. In my therapeutic process, I learned the importance of writing in order to be able to heal. While I was writing this chapter, I noticed my growth and how much I am recovering from my painful past. I recognize that I can not control what I endured. However, I can control my course of action in the present moment. In therapy, I also developed awareness about how necessary it is to work with consistency to improve some old habits that do not help me to evolve and be the best version of myself.

In addition, I have been processing my grief. Some people might think that grieving or mourning are just necessary when a family member dies. In my recovery journey, I found that I could feel sorrow when a part of me died because somehow I decided to let go of the ingenuous young woman. Transformation is imperative but painful at the same time. I also gained an understanding of how to stop focusing on my level of motivation to make things happen. Antonio Machado once said: "Traveler, there is no road; you make your own path as you walk". I accepted that challenge to face any feeling that stops me from maintaining my life's commitment. Certainly, we all have emotions and we can not allow them to control us. That is why, I wake up determined to fulfill my role as a CEO and show up for my clients;

even when I am not in the mood to do it. This is because I am in control of my emotional state. And as an owner of my company, I must be responsible and dedicated to prosper.

During sessions, I realized that discipline is when you keep a balance between a rational and an emotional mind. And that is how self-determination flourishes. And I am resolved to continue my life's adventure not comparing with anyone, but to embrace that my path is unique and wonderful. In my psychological treatment, I have been able to develop a broad perspective about what dedication means for me. Some people might differ from me, but I could be successful and not a millionaire person. I consider myself a person who lives in abundance because of my experiences, the places that I go, my balanced health and life, etc. Honestly, I made peace with my own terms and I tend to challenge any dogma that states how to be happy. At the end of the day, to live with joy and satisfaction you could just leave a legacy with the positive impact that you bring to this world. I do not mean that it will not be nice to have a 6 or 7 figures business within the next year or so. At the present moment, I feel content with where I am and who I am. This is how I practice radical acceptance and the best way for me to feel peace of mind. I should highlight that I made my vision board recently and I have some amazing plans for the future. One of my objectives is to continue working with my therapist to conquer my fear of public speaking. One step at a time, I believe in myself. However, therapy has helped fulfill my purpose.

For me, working with my therapist has been helpful in mending my heart. Especially because some voices impacted me negatively since my childhood. It is true that our identities are formed according to the values that our family taught us, and our lives are influenced by what they tell us. It is evident that our identities might be fragmented if we grow up with people who present unhealthy life patterns. On top of that, facing bullying and rejection in my middle school years, fed my insecurities. Therefore, mental health therapy has been crucial in my life to confront all the voices from my past. The voices that for a long time made me feel that I was not worth it. Now I can say that I am not traveling with "old suitcases anymore". I regain my personal strength, and I can move forward to build my bright future.

## Steps to Build a Bright Future After Abuse

As I mentioned before, I was a survivor of Domestic Violence (DV). I did not figure out that I was overcoming an abusive relationship until I got hired to be a counselor for victims of DV in August 2018. It was the most difficult eye-opener and triggering work experience. I had to face all the different challenges related to the broken court system as well. However, there were some steps that I navigated to build up my determination to make it worth living life.

Here is my advice:

1. Find support because you are not alone. It is true that after abuse survivors do not necessarily have friends or family members willing to be supportive. But I found my team, including a church pastor, counselor, case manager, care coordinator, advocate, attorney, and other community supporters.

2. Expand your network. This is an ongoing process but is necessary to get out of your comfort zone. Being a survivor can make us feel vulnerable and can make it difficult to trust again. The most important existential question here is, when did you see that a seed will grow in a comfortable bed? Remember that social media is an excellent tool to start with.

3. As I mentioned before, build up your resilience. We need to believe that we have the inner strength to overcome difficult circumstances. Mental health therapy could be helpful to develop healthy coping skills and evaluate positive strategies,

including radical acceptance, mindfulness, frustration tolerance, etc.

4. Improve your cognitive flexibility and be willing to develop an optimist point of view. This is about having a fresh perspective on how the given situation could help us to personally grow and evolve. DBT therapy might be helpful if you are dealing with cognitive rigidity.

5. Learn to practice emotional intelligence. Sometimes, it is challenging to know how to control and/or understand your emotions. Developing self-awareness, self-regulation, empathy, and social skills are fundamental to thriving and building up a successful business.

6. Be proactive and realistic with your goals. Sometimes you might need to take baby steps. But just do something to start building your worth living life.

7. Solution-focused skills and stress management are essential. Of course, it is crucial to develop a risk management plan for personal and professional life. But, never get stuck thinking about possible risks. Then, anxiety could get a hold of you and not allow you to prosper.

8. Learn from mistakes and cultivate self-compassion. Being an entrepreneur is not a set of skills that you learn overnight.

9. Never stop learning, but also do not allow yourself to be pushed down by imposter syndrome. Remember how strong and powerful you are.

10. Just be genuine and be yourself. You are an unstoppable woman who faced adversity with courage. And if you survived terrible circumstances, nothing could stop you now.

## In Conclusion

Today I recognize that I am a promising Latina, female entrepreneur. I found my inner strength through the love of Jesus Christ. I decided to open my heart and mind to new possibilities. It took a huge amount of courage to break the glass ceiling. It is not easy to do, but it is not impossible to remove those invisible barriers that stop many females from becoming successful entrepreneurs. Finally, I honor the time you took to read this chapter. If you are currently facing abuse, I hope God gives you the strength and/or necessary resources to leave that unhealthy relationship. If you recently left as a survivor, I wish that you find purpose and meaning in your life. If you consider yourself a thriver, I would like this piece of advice to motivate you to become an entrepreneur. To my fellow entrepreneurs, I am glad that you had the audacity to dismantle the oppressive system and focus on your ambitions even when the world told you that you would be unable to build your bright future. Thanks for reading, and I wish you the best of luck on your journey.

## Francine Juhlin

Founder of Personal Change Warriors LLC.

https://www.linkedin.com/in/francine-juhlin-b9839578/
https://www.facebook.com/PersonalChangeWarriors
https://www.instagram.com/francinejuhlin/
https://personalchangewarriors.com/
https://personalchangewarriors.com/blog

Francine Juhlin, known as the Warrior Princess of Personal Change, endured a remarkable transformation from a worrier to a superhero in the field of personal development. With a career spanning three decades as an aircraft electrician across the Navy, Army, Government Contracting, Civil Service, and as a manufacturing engineer, Francine's journey is truly inspiring. Drawing on her expertise in industrial and corporate change management, she embarked on a quest that resulted in the creation of the 6-Step Process of Personal Change.

Applying this process to her transition into retirement, Francine gained the confidence to venture into entrepreneurship. She encourages fellow entrepreneurs to enhance their business communication strategies, opening the doors to a vibrant and prosperous entrepreneurial journey. Francine discovered that transforming your business narrative into a captivating adventure resonates with audiences, fostering meaningful connections. Her story is a testament to overcoming self-doubt and embracing a life filled with unwavering confidence.

# VANQUISHING BOOM SO YOU CAN SPARKLE

By Francine Juhlin

In the journey of becoming an unstoppable woman entrepreneur, self-confidence stands as the cornerstone of success. It is not just a desirable trait; it is the force that propels you forward, allowing you to face challenges head-on and turn setbacks into opportunities. A lack of confidence can cast a shadow on the brightest entrepreneurial prospects, from missed opportunities and indecisiveness to strained relationships and burnout.

At one time or another, we must grapple with the enigmatic presence of a pervasive inner voice—an intangible echo that reverberates within the corridors of our consciousness. This voice is not rational. This voice does not offer empirical evidence. This voice thrives on the fertile soil of our insecurities and encourages our worst instincts. In our quest for survival, this voice assumes the role of guide, a shapeshifter weaving its influence through the intricate tapestry of our thoughts. Yet, its counsel is not a beacon of wisdom; rather, it is a capricious force that can either fortify our resilience or, paradoxically, amplify our vulnerabilities.

This little voice known as BOOM – Bad Opinion of Myself – is an irrational force, devoid of proof thriving on our insecurities and fostering our worst instincts. As humans, we possess a remarkable adaptability that, over time, transforms BOOM's constant presence from novelty to mere background noise. Gradually, you cease to question its nagging and put-downs. You accept them at face value.

BOOM can lead to indecision, or what I call analysis paralysis. Is your inability to decide because you are afraid of failing? Fear of failure can hinder innovation and growth. BOOM can stifle creativity and prevent innovative ideas, leaving your business in shambles. Your potential clients, employees, and partners can feel your nervousness and lack of confidence. When you fail (and face it, we all do occasionally), your BOOM can magnify the impact of the setback. BOOM leads to stress and burnout!

Public speaking, an integral aspect of the entrepreneurial journey, is an arena where the influence of BOOM can be unmistakable. The mere thought of standing before an audience, articulating ideas, and presenting oneself can evoke a sense of terror. The fear of judgment, the worry about not being articulate enough, or the dread of stumbling over words can be overwhelming.

However, as an unstoppable woman entrepreneur, it is crucial to recognize that public speaking is not just a desirable skill but a necessary one. Whether it is pitching your business to potential investors, delivering a compelling presentation to clients, or speaking at industry conferences, effective communication is a linchpin in establishing your presence and authority in the entrepreneurial landscape.

The fear associated with public speaking often stems from BOOM's irrational whispers, magnifying insecurities and playing on the fear of judgment. Yet, overcoming this fear is imperative for several reasons. Essentially, public speaking allows you to showcase your expertise, ideas, and passion for your entrepreneurial endeavors. It is an opportunity to connect with your audience, build trust, and leave a lasting impression.

Moreover, public speaking is a powerful tool for networking and building relationships. It enables you to engage with potential clients, collaborators, and partners, opening doors to new opportunities and collaborations. In a world where connections play a pivotal role in business success, the ability to communicate effectively in public settings becomes a strategic advantage.

While the fear of public speaking may persist, it is essential to view it as a hurdle that, once overcome, can significantly contribute to personal and professional growth. Developing this skill not only boosts your self-confidence but also positions you as a confident and authoritative leader in your industry.

Conquering the fear of public speaking requires practice, preparation, and a shift in mindset. Recognizing that BOOM's negative opinions are unfounded and that people deserve to hear your voice can be a transformative realization. Embracing public speaking as a necessary and empowering aspect of your entrepreneurial journey will not only enhance your communication skills but also propel you toward becoming an unstoppable woman entrepreneur, confidently navigating the challenges that come your way.

Let us look at a case study to see how we can overcome such difficulties. Here we will see what BOOM caused in Trina's life and how Trina vanquished BOOM.

Once upon a time in a town like many others, an entrepreneur named Trina Trepidation had a brilliant mind for business, but unfortunately, her BOOM was as vast as the universe, and it was causing her entrepreneurial endeavors to spiral into a cosmic catastrophe. Trina's office was a curious mix of Post-it notes with brilliant ideas and a collection of Magic 8-balls that she consulted religiously before making any decisions. Her indecision was legendary, earning her the nickname "Trina the Trembler."

One day, Trina had a groundbreaking idea for a product that could revolutionize the market. It was a sock-tracking service that would help people find their lost socks. Users would simply register their socks with a microelectronic tracker, and if one went missing, they could put the tracking number in the database and find their sock on the map. However, as Trina began to develop the concept, her BOOM crept in like a mischievous business partner.

*Will the technology be easy enough for people to understand? Is this sustainable? Could she manage the team required to pull this off? Which supplier will produce enough trackers? Oh, the agony of choice!*

Trina's analysis paralysis kicked in, and she found herself spending days debating the pros and cons of every tiny detail. Her employees were confused and distracted by the constant indecision. Meanwhile, her potential investors who heard about her groundbreaking idea and wanted in started to lose interest. Trina's fear of failure was contagious, spreading like wildfire through the marketplace.

Her office soon became a chaotic mess of discarded prototypes and rejected designs. Trina was so afraid of presenting her project to potential investors that she decided to keep the presentation as short as possible and concentrate on design features. The once-enthusiastic employees, catching Trina's nervous vibes, started second-guessing their decisions and questioning the viability of the sock identifier.

Trina's potential business partners were also feeling the jitters. Every meeting with Trina turned into a comedy of errors with awkward silences and uncomfortable glances. Trina was so unsure of herself that she could not articulate the benefits of her invention, why it is useful, and why everyone in the world needs to be using it. She nervously read a specification sheet filled with industry jargon and acronyms that even she had trouble understanding. Nobody felt the power and possibilities of what sat in front of them. Like attracts like, they say, and in Trina's case, nervousness was the new business strategy. As the pressure mounted, Trina faced a setback. Investors started backing out of the deal. Trina's BOOM magnified the impact of this disaster.

Feeling the weight of the world on her shoulders, Trina found herself succumbing to burnout and stress, the toll evident in her once-lustrous hair now turned gray. Her healthy skin looked like she was going through puberty again. She was sure that an ulcer was forming in her gut. In the end, Trina's fear of failure had cast a shadow over her business and health, rendering them as uncertain as her own confidence. Trina Trepidation, the entrepreneur who doubted herself into oblivion, serves as a cautionary tale for aspiring businesspeople everywhere.

Trina was sick and tired of being sick and tired. She could not remember the last time she got a full night of sleep and ate a meal that did not end with heartburn. She sat in her office and experienced a full-blown meltdown. The feeling of incompetence made Trina focus on the negatives, blaming herself for everything that went wrong. As she contemplated her situation, Trina knew that something had to change.

In a pivotal realization, Trina begrudgingly acknowledged her need for help. As she cautiously consulted a new coach, Trina could not have anticipated the profound impact this decision would have on her business slump. The coach, far from merely assisting in drafting a marketing plan, delivered a resounding wake-up call that reverberated through the foundation of Trina's complacency. The pressing need for a transformative shift in her mindset became extremely obvious. The coach helped Trina craft a strategic roadmap to dismantle the formidable barriers impeding Trina's progress. This was not merely a plan; it was a blueprint for dismantling the formidable barriers standing between Trina and success. With her roadmap and unwavering determination, Trina began her radical transformation.

The initial step was for Trina to view herself as a winner. Overcoming self-doubt began with visualization—she had to imagine achieving success, envision the positive impact on her life, and experience the emotions tied to that accomplishment. Visualization created a mental roadmap guiding actions and strengthening belief in her capabilities. Following this, Trina embraced a healthy dose of self-awareness.

Trina's journey stands as a powerful testament to the transformative impact of acknowledging one's vulnerabilities, actively seeking guidance, and fearlessly embarking on the path to personal and professional development. At the heart of her remarkable story lie the crucial initial steps she took through self-awareness exercises. Self-awareness served as the compass that illuminated the shadows of her limiting belief system, which had long confined her to a state of mere survival. Recognizing the profound impact of her mindset, she courageously committed to dismantling those barriers, allowing the seeds of personal growth to take root. Trina's story underscores the profound truth that recognizing one's vulnerabilities is not a sign of weakness but rather a courageous acknowledgment of the areas ready for transformation.

Trina's initial attempt at self-awareness involved a thorough evaluation of her strengths and weaknesses. While challenging, she compiled a list of her strengths, beginning with her college degree and job experiences. A lighthearted moment arose as she recalled receiving the award for "most likely to succeed" in high school. To her surprise, Trina discovered that her accomplishments far outweighed her setbacks.

A pivotal shift occurred when Trina started viewing what she once perceived as failures as valuable learning opportunities. Reflecting on her recent sock identifier project, she meticulously listed everything that went awry. Upon careful consideration, she refined the list to five key items. Trina recognized that her inclination to micromanage frustrated her team. She acknowledged the negative impact of analysis paralysis on seizing opportunities. Trina also realized she had neglected communication with potential investors and struggled to articulate her innovative ideas due to a fear of public speaking. Notably, she identified the biggest personal limitation as BOOM. BOOM's irrational whispers magnified her insecurities, making small setbacks appear to be major failures.

Embracing the notion that failures are opportunities for improvement, Trina diligently followed her coach's plan. With newfound self-awareness, she delved into practical strategies for overcoming confidence barriers. From adopting a mindset that sees failure as a stepping stone to success, addressing BOOM's erroneous behavior, to cultivating self-compassion, these actionable tips empowered Trina to navigate challenges and bolster her confidence.

Hidden strengths lie within us, waiting to emerge. It often takes failures (learning experiences) to uncover them. Trina's failure became her most significant opportunity for future success. Failures are valuable lessons waiting for you to discover. Trina discovered crucial lessons: she needed to have faith in herself before expecting others to have faith in her. Effective communication is a potent tool in the entrepreneur's arsenal. Being able to tell a compelling story would help Trina become not only an unstoppable woman entrepreneur but also empower her team to unleash their full potential. Confidence is not just a trait; it is a superpower waiting for you to harness for extraordinary entrepreneurial success.

Imagine if Trina told a story about a lost sock and how the tracker helped it find its partner rather than reading a specification sheet filled with industry jargon and acronyms. Nobody connected with her failed attempt to win over the potential investors. Her initial communication was boring and confusing to the people. A story would have captured their attention, and the investors would have been able to envision the possibilities. Trina learned that there are eight elements to an engaging story, and she crafted her new sock story with these elements as a guide.

**Define the characters**. Mr. and Mrs. Sockatellie were a happy couple. They belonged to a little girl named Jane who went to summer camp. Jane's mom packed the Sockatelli couple with Jane's camping gear and sent Jane off for two weeks of fun in the woods.

**What do the characters desire?** Mr. and Mrs. Sockatellie were proud of their job. They had the important mission of keeping Jane's feet warm and protecting them from the shoes which have been known to cause blisters. The Sockatellie couple wanted nothing more than to ensure that Jane's feet were safe and comfortable.

**What is stopping the desire?** Upon Jane's return home from camp, Jane's mom was horrified that Mr. Sockatellie was all alone. Where did the Mrs. go?

**Create tension.** Mr. Sockatellie became withdrawn and anxious. Not only was his partner missing, but he also could not fulfill his mission. He worried about Jane's little feet.

**Provide rich imagery.** As winter blew in, there was a bone-chilling cold. Jane's sock drawer was missing one of her favorite pair of socks. Jane saw Mr. Sockatellie sitting in the drawer, not realizing that the worst-case scenario was about to occur. The Sockatellies were her most comfortable socks. Jane missed them terribly. If only she made sure that Mrs. Sockatellie was in her laundry bag when she left camp.

**Share the emotion.** The next day, Jane cried because she got a "C" on a test. Instead of eating her lunch, Jane vented to her friends. Her friends listened to her story about how her feet were cold, and she could not concentrate during the test.

**Hook them with a change of direction.** When Emma learned that Jane lost a favorite sock, she told her friend all about her sock trackers. Emma left one of her socks behind at camp too. Emma's mom was able to plug the tracking number into the database on the Track Your Socks website. A flashing red dot appeared on the map, showing the location of the camp's lost and found. Her favorite sock was retrieved.

**Give a treasure.** Jane told her mom about Emma's sock tracker. Hoping that Mrs. Sockatellie suffered the same fate as Emma's sock, Jane's mom called the camp and found that YES INDEED, Mrs. Sockatellie was in the lost and found. After Mrs. Sockatellie's safe return, Jane's mom ordered trackers for all the socks the family owned.

After refining the story with her coach, Trina embraced the storytelling task with the same enthusiasm as a children's librarian leading a story hour, injecting the narrative with vibrant energy and emotion. Guided by her coach, she mastered the art of using vocal variety and nonverbal communication to bring her characters to life, weaving a tapestry of emotions that deeply resonated with her audience and left a lasting impact on their hearts and minds. During the part of the story when Jane discovers her "C" grade, Trina's body language reflected the disappointment of a young girl on the verge of tears. With each practice session, Trina found increasing joy in sharing the story. Armed with a captivating story and polished delivery, she felt well-prepared to revisit potential investors.

On the pivotal day of Trina's second opportunity to impress potential investors, she took a moment to reflect on her list of strengths and opportunities that she wrote what seemed like ages ago, reminding herself of the considerable progress she had made since feeling like a failure. With a clear mind and a sense of readiness, she embarked on the challenge ahead. Trina began the meeting by sharing a captivating story about the socks. After delivering the emotional ending, she engaged the audience by asking if they had ever experienced the loss of a favorite sock, prompting them to recall the "emotional turmoil of cold feet on test day." Trina did not need to say much more; each potential investor was poised to sign a contract, sensing the profound impact this venture could have on the world.

Trina vanquished BOOM with unwavering determination! The seismic shift in her life compelled her to shed the moniker "Trina Trepidation" and embrace the resounding title of "Trina the Tranquil." Not only did she salvage her business, but Trina's triumph also soared to unimaginable heights, eclipsing even her wildest dreams.

Is BOOM stopping you from telling your story effectively? How might a spellbinding narrative revolutionize the impact of your business? Imagine evoking emotional engagement from your audience. What messages could a memorable brand story convey to potential customers, employees, and investors? Picture yourself standing out in a competitive landscape, leaving a lasting impression.

In the vivacious journey to becoming an unstoppable woman entrepreneur, the key to unlocking your full potential lies in mastering the art of self-confidence. Taming the relentless bully that is your inner voice, or BOOM, is the pivotal first step toward cultivating the unshakable confidence needed to propel you toward unprecedented success. As you delve into the depths of understanding your strengths and opportunities, you equip yourself with the armor to transform setbacks into stepping stones for growth.

The threat of a confidence deficit looms ominously, casting shadows over the brightest entrepreneurial prospects. Now, as you stand at this crossroads, the call to action is clear – seek the guidance of a coach. A coach's perspective is valuable because they can often see strengths, skills, and abilities in you that are hidden by your BOOM's ugly, whispered words. Find a guiding light to lead you through the maze of challenges, enabling you to emerge not just as a successful entrepreneur, but as an empowered and unstoppable force ready to conquer the limitless possibilities that await. Find the courage to step out of your comfort zone and take on the challenges that BOOM has been telling you to avoid so that you can discover superpowers that will set you on an extraordinary trajectory toward unlimited success.

## Marissa Warren

Marissa Warren
Hypnotherapist & Transformational Consultant

### Marissa Warren Linkedin

https://www.linkedin.com/in/marissawarren-hypnotherapist-transformationalconsultant/

### Marissa Warren Facebook

https://www.facebook.com/marissa.warren.transformational

### Marissa Warren Instagram

https://www.instagram.com/marissawarren_/

**Marissa Warren**
https://www.marissawarren.com/

**Marissa Warren Courses**
https://bit.ly/MarissaWarrenCourses

Marissa is a hypnotherapist and transformational consultant working with RTT – Rapid Transformational Therapy, QHHT – Quantum Healing Hypnosis Technique, Somatic and Tantric embodiment, breathwork and sound healing.

Marissa embodies these modalities in her life and have used these to heal trauma, make major changes, create transformations and align to her soul's and life's purpose.

For those ready to reclaim inner freedom, break free from past limitations, step into their best life, take action, are ready to uplevel and elevate their life, want to achieve true transformations, and realign with their souls' purpose and align to their own unique authenticity and sovereignty – Marissa is the transformational consultant to help!

Leaving you feeling empowered, living from infinite inner power and potential and stepping into the life and level of success you desire, Marissa will help you tap into your inner magic and utilise your inner resources to step up and shine.

# BREAK FREE

By Marissa Warren

### Release the inner Critic:
*"How to escape imposter syndrome and step into visibility success"*

"I feel stuck!"

"I don't want to live like this anymore!"

"But every time I want to do something I think, what will they say or do?!"

These were the thoughts I used to think that kept me stuck in analysis paralysis. I knew that I wanted to move forward in my life and in the business I had at the time, but it felt like a big, heavy block inside of me was stopping me from moving forward and taking action. I wanted to step up and be seen but I felt like no matter what I did, nothing was working! Everything just felt off energetically…

I was so caught up in my head about what I thought other people would say about me if I did something to be visible and put myself out there. I let the inner critic in me take over. I created false narratives about other people that I thought were true but I didn't have any factual evidence for them – it was all in my head! I let these stories and belief systems control my life, which ultimately led me to burnout and complete overwhelm! I was absolutely sabotaging my success before I even had a chance to fully achieve it. It was exhausting and isolating, but I couldn't see any other way out; there was no key to the lock on the cage I had boxed myself in.

Fast forward to where I am now and it feels like a distant, unrecognisable past version of myself. However, without this experience, I wouldn't be where I am today. It was through this experience that I was able to turn that pain into purpose and fuel for my inner fire.

Hi, I'm Marissa Warren, a hypnotherapist and transformational consultant working with RTT or Rapid Transformational Therapy – a combination of NLP (neurolinguistic programming), CBT (cognitive behavioural therapy), hypnotherapy, and psychotherapy- as well as QHHT or Quantum Healing Hypnosis Technique – past life regression, Somatic, and Tantric embodiment, Breathwork, and Sound healing. I am also a keynote speaker and author.

Throughout the many experiences in my life, I feel like my journey has been an "all roads lead to the right path," and it is due to my extensive skills and experience that I am able to deeply tap into and access the parts of my clients that are needed for deep healing, shifts, and uplevels.

When I was younger, I had a deep trauma occur that was a sliding doors moment for me. It led to a series of decisions, actions, beliefs, and behaviours that became embedded in me for a lifetime. But I pushed that event down so deep; it was so far removed from my conscious memory. Yet my subconscious remembered and was playing this out through false stories and narratives for so long, causing me to repeat behaviours that were not aligned with me living my best life.

Then, three years ago, I experienced a life-defining moment with the passing of my father, leading me to make major changes in my life. I went on a soul journey, and my life has never been the same since. I implemented all the tools and resources that I use with my clients, I did the deep inner work and transformed my life - stepping into the role of being a master creator, designer, and manifester of my life, being able to achieve amazing shifts and transformations in a short period of time.

Working through trauma, overcoming burnout, and facing a few major life events have all been catalysts for moving me into alignment with my soul's passion and purpose. It is these experiences and my life journey that help me to be able to understand my clients on a deeper level.

It is my passion to help others elevate themselves to achieve more in life, break free from past experiences and limitations, and step into living the life they truly desire. Seeing the transformations that my clients experience is what lights my soul on fire.

## Recognizing Imposter Syndrome

A pivotal and defining moment for me during my business evolution was finally being able to rewrite the inner narrative and stop letting the inner critic take over. I went on a deep soul and inward journey to the depths of myself and felt that once I was able to meet all parts of myself with acceptance, kindness, and compassion, there was nothing that anyone could do or say that would even come close to the depths I had persecuted myself with the negative narrative I had been living by.

My imposter syndrome was so strong and it played out in ways I didn't even realise! It showed up due to constant content consumption, course after course, which caused me not to show up and be seen or express my wants and needs. I was not able to be an advocate for myself, didn't assert my boundaries, and felt like I needed to be a chameleon and everything to everyone else while I was depleting myself. I ended up being nothing for myself and keeping myself playing small – stuck at the same level – craving more but unable to move toward it.

Imposter syndrome is a silent attacker, lying dormant behind the scenes, and just when you think you are ready to uplevel and move forward to a new experience in life or work, it comes up to take over the show.

The thing with imposter syndrome is that you could be suffering from it and not even realise it!

*How do you know if you have imposter syndrome? Do you feel…*

- Fear of being exposed as a fraud

- Fear of failure
- Like no matter what you do it's never good enough
- Unworthy of the success you have achieved
- High levels of self-doubt
- An inability to celebrate success
- Lack of acknowledgement of success
- Negative inner dialogue
- Like you are setting extremely high standards

How many do you resonate with? If you have found one or more, it could be a good chance that you have a layer of imposter syndrome sneaking around in your subconscious mind. Your subconscious mind is the processes, behaviours, thoughts, actions, and information that you are not consciously aware of. These are the automatic responses, habits, and emotions that operate below the conscious mind.

No one is immune to this; it can affect many people from all professions and careers. Even mothers feel this and constantly judge their parenting choices and feel guilt over what they are or aren't doing for their children. Imposter syndrome is a very real experience that many suffer from in silence, or don't even know that is what is contributing to their current life and professional experiences.

There are many effects of imposter syndrome which can include:

*Analysis paralysis*

This is the inability to take action or make a decision. You know you need to make a decision and take action but it all feels too hard or you don't have any clarity to make the right decision.

*Avoidance of pursuing opportunities*

Avoiding taking on new opportunities or responsibilities; fearing that you will not be able to handle these or that you may be exposed as undeserving or unworthy.

*Burnout*

The pressure to meet unrealistic standards and the constant fear of being discovered as an impostor can contribute to burnout. Overworking to prove yourself may lead to physical and mental exhaustion. You may feel that you need to do more and do it all or that no one else can do the job as well as you can so you end up depleting yourself in the process of proving your self-worth and self-value.

*Career Limitations*

In a professional environment, impostor syndrome could harmfully limit career advancement. It could lead to you not pursuing any promotions or leadership roles, even if you are qualified, due to a lack of confidence in your skills and abilities.

*Feeling like opportunities are not achievable or possible for you*

You may feel like success and life is happening to everyone else except you. You can't understand why other people are having all of these amazing results and nothing seems to be working out for you. It feels like life is happening to you and not for you.

*Heightened feelings of self-doubt, unworthiness and not feeling good enough*

You could have a strong inner dialogue of negative self-talk that is holding you back from believing in yourself enough to put yourself out there and take chances in life. The words you tell yourself could be so terrible that you would never say them to another person, so why say them to yourself?

*Inability to celebrate success and milestones*

How often do you stop to celebrate the wins along the way? Life is a journey, not a destination, and it is who you become in the process and the elevations you embody throughout the experiences. The more you celebrate your successes and wins, the easier it is to call in more of these experiences because you are moving into becoming a vibrational and energetic alignment to success. The more success you celebrate, the more it affirms your worthiness of more success.

## Increased stress and anxiety

Constantly doubting yourself and worrying about being exposed as not experienced enough or worthy can contribute to increased levels of stress and anxiety. This can have negative effects on both mental and physical health.

## Lacking in confidence

Impostor syndrome often leads to a lack of confidence in your abilities. This can affect your willingness to take on new challenges or pursue growth opportunities. All this leads to is feeling stuck and not moving forward in life.

## Procrastination

Fear of not meeting high standards or being exposed as a fraud can lead to procrastination. You may delay tasks due to anxiety about your self-perceived lack of competence, skill level, knowledge, or expertise.

## Setting impossibly high standards for yourself and others

If you feel that nothing anyone does is ever good enough or that you need to do everything yourself, it could be imposter syndrome showing up. Release the pursuit for perfection, alleviate the pressure from yourself and others, and embrace others' uniqueness and abilities.

## Strained relationships

Impostor syndrome can impact relationships as you may struggle to accept praise, recognition, or acknowledgment. This could potentially lead to isolation to avoid unwanted attention or focus from others.

## Stuck in the comparison trap

Constant comparison with others can lead to feelings of inadequacy, affecting your self-esteem and contributing to a sense of not being good enough. You may feel like you are behind in life compared to others.

## How Do You Overcome Imposter Syndrome?

Overcoming imposter syndrome can be a process that involves a combination of self-awareness, inner dialogue reframing, and taking proactive steps to rebuild confidence and self-esteem. It involves self-kindness, self-compassion, self-empathy, and patience with yourself.

The first step is self-awareness. Once you can accept where you are and what your limitations are, you can be empowered to face these and rise! You are the creator of your life and the only limits are the ones you are creating for yourself.

Flip the script! If you think a negative thought, ask yourself "What is the opposite of this thought?" The more you think these new thoughts and align with them, the more they become your new normal. The more you think new thoughts, the more you are forming new neural pathways. Think of it like wearing a path down in the grass, the more you walk that same way, the more you are forming a new pathway — this is the same with your mindset and thought patterns. It is also like when you start a new fitness regime. When you first start, it feels uncomfortable and hard, but the more you persist, the easier it becomes and the more you are seeing results.

When you catch a negative thought coming into your mind, have self-awareness of the thought, acknowledge the thought, reframe the thought, and then release this thought. It is no longer needed or required and it is serving no purpose or providing any sense of fulfilment.

If you find that you have a perpetual thought that just keeps looping over and over again and is stubborn to leave, journey deeper into this thought to gain insights and clarity into why it won't leave and what purpose it feels that it is serving by staying in your head. I like to move through a series of inner questions to confirm if what I'm thinking is true and accurate. These questions are from the work of *Byron Katie. These questions are:

1. *Is it true?*

2. *Do I know it is absolutely true? Is there evidence of this?*

3. *How do I react and what happens when I believe the thought?*

4. *Who would I be without the thought? How would I show up for myself and life?*

*Make celebration a part of your daily life.* What wins can you celebrate? How can you praise and acknowledge yourself? The more you can do this, the more you can reaffirm your positive traits and successes.

*Visualise success!* When you can envision it, you can create it. Aligning with a positive mindset and future vision helps you to take positive actions and steps to work towards this.

*Don't struggle on your own.* There are people that can help you to overcome this. With the work that I do, I can get to the root cause of the issue, release this, and recode and rewire the subconscious to come into alignment with positive and self-affirming behaviours and actions.

*Release the pursuit for perfection.* Understand that perfectionism can contribute to impostor syndrome. Accept that nobody is perfect, and mistakes are opportunities for learning and growth.

*Embrace vulnerability.* When you can own all parts of yourself, you can live from a place of authenticity. This also helps to deepen your connection with others and contributes to building resilience. You are also taking your power back from imposter syndrome by not allowing it to have anything to feed on.

*Take courageous and aligned action.* This helps you to keep moving forward and rise above adversity and challenges. "Ask yourself every morning, what is one thing I can do today to move me closer to my goals?"

*Release all that no longer serves you.* What do you need to release to step into the courageous version of yourself that you want to be? When you think about the version of you that is living a life free from fear, a negative inner dialogue, and achieving the level of success that you are craving, what does this version of you look like? What thoughts do they think? How do they live their life? How do they show up in daily life?

When you can get clear on these elements, you can align energetically to this level and become a vibrational match to this new version of you.

I fully understand the journey it takes to overcome imposter syndrome and elevate to a higher level. This is something that I have moved through in my own life and understand first-hand how challenging change can be. I'm not saying that I don't still have moments where thoughts pop into my head that could have the potential to derail me, the only difference is that I have inner resources to access to overcome these, silence the inner critic, take my power back and can now move through this experience faster and easier. By being able to do the inner work, never giving up, and taking control as the creator of my life, I am now doing the work that is my soul's purpose and passion and I am living each day in full flow, ease, creativity, and bliss.

## Ready to Transform?

I also understand how hard it can be to make changes in your inner world when you have adversity in your outer world. I am here to help you break free from your inner limitations and step into living a life of inner freedom.

Enjoy a free program to overcome your imposter syndrome and become a visibility success!

You can access this via the link below. Please use the code: **BUWEFREE** when you register.

**Free Book Resources**

https://marissa-warren.mn.co/plans/378421?bundle_token=5066e3a5a392d5eb62f96640706c1d46&utm_source=manual

## Included in these bonuses:

Break free from imposter syndrome and journey on your exploration of inner reflection and self-discovery. To help you uncover your form of imposter syndrome and implement an easy action plan to make change easy, follow along with the Imposter Syndrome journal.

Please enjoy this free audio on overcoming imposter syndrome to help you along the journey to reclaim your power and break free from imposter syndrome.

You can book a free discovery call and we can discuss what is going on for you and how I can best support you to move on from where you are to where you want to be. Together we will deep dive into helping you to break free and create and step into living the life of your dreams.

**Book Free Discovery Call**

https://booknow.marissawarren.com/#/discoverycall

To connect with me further and to find out more information, please visit my website.

**Marissa Warren**

https://www.marissawarren.com/

I would love to offer you a free 5-day program – 5 DAYS TO FREEDOM. In this program, you will receive valuable tools and insights into how you can align easier with your authenticity and sovereignty to help you access your inner magic and craft your dream life.

**5 Days to Freedom FREE program**

https://marissa-warren.mn.co/plans/390885?bundle_token=
2d946f4a44c5fc8602b7bca47562da4f&utm_source=manual

*References:*
*https://thework.com/2017/10/four-liberating-questions/*

## Anne-Marie Springer

Owner of Wise Moose LLC

www.linkedin.com/in/anne-marie-springer-52958143
https://www.facebook.com/annemarie.springer.98
https://www.instagram.com/annemarie.springer/
https://wisemoosegrinds.com

Anne-Marie Springer has always had a passion for caring for others and currently works as an RN in a family practice clinic where she specializes in preventive health. Her book "Help, My Baby Won't Stop Crying! A Simple Guide for New Parents" provides clear, easy-to-follow advice for parents struggling with soothing their newborns. Her clear and easy-to-follow advice has helped many families find and use various strategies to reduce stress. Anne-Marie is an adventurer at heart, and when she's not busy taking care of patients and writing down her thoughts and ideas, she loves to explore new places, bake cookies, and cherish every moment spent with her loved ones. She and her husband have three adult children and live in Illinois with their two dogs. Anne-Marie is expanding her online coffee business, Wise Moose Grinds https://wisemoosegrinds.com, writing a fiction book for young adults, and exploring her following entrepreneurial project ideas.

# DISRUPT THE PROCRASTINATION CYCLE AND BECOME UNSTOPPABLE

By Anne-Marie Springer

Raise your hand if you have big dreams and ideas, are destined to be the next successful female entrepreneur, but struggle with procrastination. If so, you are not alone. You can break free from procrastination by identifying what causes you to procrastinate, what results from your procrastination, and what methods you can successfully use to disrupt the cycle.

## Introduction to Procrastination

People procrastinate for numerous reasons including depression, distractions, fear of failure, avoidance of criticism, perfectionism, lack of motivation, and present bias (the preference for immediate gratification over long-term rewards). Outcomes from procrastination vary widely but may include low self-esteem, low satisfaction, health problems, and missed opportunities.

Procrastination may lead to stress and anxiety from the guilt of not completing designated tasks. These feelings, in turn, lead to more pressure and urgency, affecting mood and performance. Poor performance and quality may result from the rush to finish a task at the last minute, leading to mistakes and substandard results. The good news is that there are ways to overcome the tendency and increase your satisfaction with your accomplishments.

## Overcoming Obstacles

If you are starting or have already begun your entrepreneurial journey, look closely at your goals, vision, market research, and business plans. Make sure that they are clear, specific, and realistic. Spell out what you do, what problem you will solve, and who will help you reach your goals. Establish a plan and a schedule that allows you to group tasks into manageable steps with the most urgent and vital tasks listed at the top. Motivation and focus will lead to progress and, ultimately, success. It should also help to reduce the tendency to procrastinate.

Many women have phenomenal business ideas but few realize their aspirations. Take the time to write down your ideas. Trust in yourself and your dreams, and remember, no one in the history of entrepreneurship has had an idea that was perfect from the get-go. Anne Wojcicki, co-founder of 23andMe, is known for saying, "If you want to change this world, this community we all live in, then get up and do it. And just start something."

As a nurse, I spent many hours with people at the end of their lives, and not one talked about how happy they were to have stayed in the same place, doing the same things, without ever pursuing their dreams. Life at its core is imperfect and messy. Waiting for all your ducks to line up before you start your business will most likely work out, as well as expecting the Jell-O you nailed to the wall to stay.

## Moving Forward After Loss

In November, I made a new friend; she was 35 years old, an emergency room nurse, and getting ready to attend her daughter's wedding in a few months. She passed away in her sleep the following month from a heart attack. I mention this experience because each of us has or will experience loss in our lifetimes. This can be the loss of a loved one, an ability or organ, or a loss of finances, which can lead to depression.

Don't let a loss stop you from following your dreams or taking the first steps forward in a positive direction. I know this is easier said than done, but you must continue to move forward for yourself and your loved ones. Take some time to address your loss. Acknowledge your feelings, give yourself time to heal, reach out to friends and family, seek therapy, and take care of yourself. Strive to shift thoughts away from the past and toward the positive, seek resilience, and focus on the possibilities in the future.

When my husband and I lost our first baby to Sudden Infant Death Syndrome, it was crippling, and it took some time to get past the excruciating pain of loss. We embraced our grief and sadness with support from friends and family and worked on taking care of our physical and emotional well-being. We were blessed with a beautiful baby girl two years later, followed by another girl three years later and a boy four years later. The demands of raising a young family, going to school, and working full-time can be challenging, and it is easy to put your aspirations on the back burner.

## Failure Fosters Strength

As an entrepreneur, you may often fear failure. But don't let this fear lead to procrastination. Don't worry about failing, making mistakes, losing money, or facing criticism. These are all part of the learning process. Instead of avoiding failure, embrace it as an opportunity to grow and improve. Failure is not a sign of weakness or incompetence but a chance to develop new skills and gain insights.

Debbi Fields, founder of Mrs. Fields Cookies, says, "The important thing is not being afraid to take a chance. Remember, the greatest failure is to not try. Once you find something you love to do, be the best at doing it." If you are struggling, return to the clear and specific goals you set for yourself and realign them with your vision and resources. Try to look at failure as a temporary setback, remember your positive thinking, and lean on your support system to help you overcome this potential barrier.

## Seize the Moment

As the world changes and becomes more interconnected, many new business opportunities are opening. Technology is evolving, and you have brilliant ideas and something to offer that the world needs. Cultivate confidence in your abilities and visualize your desired goals. Picture yourself overcoming any challenges and achieving your goals to improve your motivation, confidence, and creativity.

If you are waiting for the economy to improve, you may need an in with a very accurate psychic to predict what will happen with the world's complex and ever-changing economies. You may have a long wait and want to avoid starting your business during a downturn. However, now is an excellent time to begin. You will learn to adapt to circumstances and opportunities as they present themselves and find innovative and creative solutions.

## Overcoming Detractors

You will encounter people who are skeptics, pessimists, and discouragers. These are your naysayers, and they will try to convince you that your entrepreneurial ideas are misguided, stupid, unsustainable, or that you should put ketchup on a hotdog. It will be challenging, but keep this group of people from affecting your motivation, enthusiasm, or confidence. Ayn Rand, author and philosopher, says, "The question isn't who's going to let me, it's who's going to stop me."

When friends, family, or acquaintances try to discourage you from accomplishing your vision, thank them for their input and tell them you will put their suggestions on your list of pros and cons when evaluating your business plan. Consider using any negativity to increase your drive and determination. Work hard and prove them wrong. Listen to what they say, but follow your instincts, passion, and the experts in the field you are pursuing.

You may learn something valuable from your detractors for improving your business or concept. Do not be afraid to challenge their negativity and use it to validate your ideas further. Reduce the amount of contact you have with them, whether in person, by phone, email, or text.

## Focusing Amidst Chaos

One of the leading causes of procrastination is distraction. To avoid becoming distracted by things that will not add value to your life or your business like playing solitaire, staring into the refrigerator when you are not hungry, or watching a movie you have seen 20 times, consider setting up a clutter-free quiet work area. Set aside a time when you will not look at social media or other unnecessary electronics while working.

It is common knowledge that music affects mood, but scientific research has shown that some genres are better for improving cognition. Classical music may enhance your thinking, but if you find it irritating, play something that fits the occasion and your mood.

Playing music with lyrics can distract your attention from your task and reduce how much of what you are reading that you understand or recall later. Additionally, you may want to avoid music that brings out strong emotions, like ballads playing when someone you loved passed away or the tune blasting from when you first fell in love.

Try searching for and playing ambient music that helps block out noise and can help reduce stress, like *Ambient Study Music To Concentrate*. Classical music may improve reasoning and problem-solving, like *Mozart for Brain Power*. Alpha-wave music uses sound frequencies designed to match the alpha waves in your brain and may help you to be relaxed but alert with improved concentration, like *Alpha Waves Music for Concentration*.

## Conquering Procrastination With Effective Organization

You may be putting off essential activities if you feel overwhelmed by how many things you must do or how complicated your tasks are. Organize your to-do list into manageable sections with specific, achievable goals to reduce stress and increase motivation.

You may benefit from using the Pomodoro technique, a time management method where you will work on a task for 25 minutes, take a break for five minutes, and after two hours, take a more extended break of 15 to 30 minutes. This method will help you concentrate, avoid burnout, and reward yourself for accomplishing tasks.

When you start to lose focus on a task, it may lead to boredom or lack of motivation. It's important to remind yourself why you are doing the task and the potential outcomes that may result from completing or not completing it. Positive redirection should give you a little boost of motivation, help you overcome any resistance to the task, and keep you on track to reach your goals.

## Mastering Your Mindset

Some days, you may have negative thoughts that lead to procrastination like "This is just too hard," or "I will do it later." Try to replace those thoughts with thoughts like "I will do it now," or "I am up for this challenge." I admit, I tend to cry when excessively frustrated or angry (keep some soft tissues around but not the ones with lotion; they smear your glasses), but I have found that if I can clear negative thoughts, it always leads to much better outcomes. Positive thinking is a must.

When you are experiencing dread, fear, anxiety, or depression, say to yourself, "Clear and delete," and refocus on positive, happy, creative, and grateful thoughts. As Peter Pan suggested, "Just think lovely, wonderful thoughts, and they lift you up in the air." These thoughts will increase your ability to work through challenges and setbacks proactively and save money on tissues used in the event of an emotional breakdown.

## Harnessing Optimism for Success

Positivity will help keep you motivated, assist you with exploring new ideas, and find optimal solutions to any problems you may encounter. Happy and positive people come across to their peers and customers as motivated, passionate, approachable, and determined. If you can remain optimistic on most days (who doesn't have a bad day now and then), it will help you make decisions with more balance and fewer knee-jerk reactions.

Many studies that follow human emotions show that people with positive outlooks feel less stressed, are happier with their work, and have fewer problems with mental health struggles. Negative thoughts can spread through your mind like weeds in your garden. They can lead to stagnation or, even worse, destruction of motivation and productivity before your business even gets off the ground.

Use your passion and vision to help you through the hard times. If you are not passionate and ready for hard work, your odds of developing a successful enterprise may diminish as your frustration with the difficulties you encounter increases.

## Tapping Into Wisdom with Expert Guidance

Successful entrepreneurs often advise new business owners to surround themselves with successful, positive, knowledgeable people with skills that complement the business. Allow experts in their fields to give you honest feedback and criticism, and challenge yourself not to become defensive or angry.

You will need help. Surround yourself with people who believe in you and will support you. Use social media, internet sites, friends, and acquaintances to help you find networking, mentors, and skilled people to guide, advise, and serve as sounding boards for your ideas. Find people in similar niches as yours, get to know them, and discover what opportunities, resources, and communities they recommend.

## Prioritizing Well-Being

Remember to care for yourself and your family as you work on your new business. Any new job can be stressful and demanding, but when you are responsible for every aspect of your new business, it is easy to feel overwhelmed. Maintaining a balance between work and personal life will benefit your health, self-actualization, motivation, and success.

Spend time with family, relax, set boundaries, prioritize tasks, take breaks, stay hydrated, eat healthy (at least most of the time), and ask for help when needed. These things will help you focus, stay productive, and avoid burnout while enhancing productivity.

## Triumphing Over Boundaries for Unbounded Success

"Everything you want is just outside your comfort zone," is a quote from businessman Robert G. Allen. If true, you must overcome fears, procrastination, and limitations and step outside your familiar routines and comfort zones to face new challenges and opportunities. When you do, you will learn and grow as an entrepreneur, and achieving your goals and manifesting your dreams will be within reach.

I know what procrastination looks like. There was always one more thing I needed to accomplish before I could sit down and write my book or start my business. It took me 56 years to start my first business, Wise Moose Grinds, and 57 years to write my first book, *Help, My Baby Won't Stop Crying!*

And now, as I continue my battle with cancer like so many other courageous women before me, I remain hopeful and refuse to have any regrets. I am proud to have spent 25 years serving my country and to now care for others who also served their country. I have experienced so many breathtakingly beautiful and awe-inspiring moments with my husband, children, friends, patients, co-workers, and acquaintances. I wouldn't change a thing.

I have only just started my journey as an entrepreneur but I am well on my way. Join me on the journey to break free from procrastination and become an unstoppable entrepreneur. I can't wait to see you surrounded with abundance as you shine a light on the world with your inspiration, ideas, and solutions.

## Sylvia Becker-Hill

Founder of Becker-Hill Inc.

https://www.linkedin.com/in/sylviabeckerhill/
https://www.facebook.com/sylvia.beckerhill/
https://www.instagram.com/sylviabeckerhill/
www.becker-hill.com
www.sylviabecker-hill.com

Sylvia Becker-Hill is a true Renaissance woman, a multiple-published bestselling author, and a seasoned edutainer who has empowered thousands of corporate executives, women leaders, and entrepreneurs around the world since 1997. In 2002, she became the first German coach to earn the coveted title of Professional Certified Coach from the International Coach Federation, establishing herself as a pioneer in the coaching world. Her impressive educational background boasts two university degrees, while her portfolio showcases over 30 certifications in various change modalities, including her accreditation as one of the world's first 10 Certified Master Neuroplasticians in 2023.

Sylvia's mission is to empower you with all the knowledge, tools, and lasting transformation you need to "FLIP" everything that bothers, hurts, or blocks you from living your desires and dreams into unquestionable Freedom, unconditional Love, envisioned Identity, and impactful Power.

Are you ready to discover the joy of feeling unabashedly alive and powerful?

# FLIP YOUR BLINDSPOTS INTO BILLIONS: TURNING FRUSTRATION INTO FREEDOM FROM SELF-SABOTAGE

By Sylvia Becker-Hill

*"We businesswomen are trained to deny feeling frustrated because it is seen as a sign of failing. It is not! As soon we stop feeling ashamed of this powerful emotion and explore it, we can flip any painful situation like a pancake into something useful."*
— Sylvia Becker-Hill

## The Problem:

Brilliant, well-trained women entrepreneurs often struggle with patterns of self-sabotage to achieve their goals, despite their best efforts. This can lead to financial drain, health collapse, and deep, painful frustration, putting them in danger of giving up. Over 45% of all start-ups fail in the USA in the first five years, and 20% are already gone by the end of year two!

This problem stems from a 'hidden side of the business' not addressed by business schools, advisors, and mentors: beliefs, vows, and emotional patterns hidden in the businesswomen's subconscious mind. Those hidden patterns are **dangerous blind spots**. Those blind spots stay hidden because their biggest red flag trying to get our attention is a strong emotion that feels 'icky' in us and is labeled by society as 'hysterical,' 'ugly,' and as a sign of failure. This emotion is FRUSTRATION.

**No businesswoman wants to be a frustrated woman! So we deny it.**
We suppress the red flags that have the power to 'lead us home'. Home within ourselves, where we can discover our truth and what is really behind our self-sabotage.

## The ABC of Self-Sabotage™

Take a moment to ground yourself inside your body utilizing deep breathing before reading the following list. Ideally, you have a pen at hand to tick off the boxes of the self-sabotage patterns you can sense you are doing. Please take your time and truly sense the meaning of each pattern and where you resonate with it in your body.

## Have you ever experienced...?

- ☐ **A**pproval seeking, despite being confident in the eyes of others?
- ☐ **A**pologizing frequently, despite hating seeing other women doing it frequently?
- ☐ **A**ssuming the worst, despite any tangible indicators in reality?

- ☐ **B**elittling past success, despite others admiring you for it?
- ☐ **B**itching, despite your promise to yourself not to?
- ☐ **B**ody hatred, despite consciously taking care of your body and trying to love it?
- ☐ **B**ullying, despite knowing the pain it causes because you got bullied too?

- ☐ **C**hasing shiny objects, despite wasting a lot of money and time on them?
- ☐ **C**omparing yourself with others, despite knowing that it doesn't serve you?

☐ Disconnecting from others, despite longing for friendship, love, and intimacy?

☐ Distracting yourself, despite craving focus and finally finishing things?

☐ Endangering your health, despite knowing your health is the foundation for success in all areas of your life?

☐ Forgetting to celebrate progress, despite knowing that it is good for you?

☐ Gossiping, despite judging other women for doing that?

☐ Hiding, despite feeling called to share your message?

☐ Ignoring achievements, despite having worked so hard for them?

☐ Ignoring your intuition, despite desiring to live in integrity with yourself?

☐ Imposter syndrome, despite consciously knowing it is not real?

☐ Fear of failure, despite accepting that failures are stepping stones to success?

☐ Fear of success, despite wanting nothing more?

☐ Following new fads, despite not having implemented the last one fully?

☐ Neglecting self-care, despite knowing you are the most important asset in your business?

☐ Not enforcing existing boundaries, despite knowing it undermines the respect of others, your perceived value, and your confidence?

☐ Not feeling like being enough, despite having done a ton of self-development work and healing of past issues yet not being able to shake this feeling off?

- ☐ **O**bsessive worrying, despite it increasing anxiety and stress?
- ☐ **O**veranalyzing, despite it not helping and leading to procrastination?
- ☐ **O**vercommitting, despite knowing you are doomed to disappoint others and yourself while creating stress for everyone?
- ☐ **O**verextending, despite knowing your resources of time, energy, and money are limited and you are creating danger for yourself?
- ☐ **O**versexualizing, despite despising patriarchal tactics wherein other women utilize their bodies to gain advantages?

- ☐ **P**eople pleasing, despite having committed to do things for yourself?
- ☐ **P**erfectionism, despite knowing how productive the attitude of "good enough" is to propel your business forward?
- ☐ **P**laying doormat, despite having worked on your self-worth, dignity, and confidence?
- ☐ **P**laying dumb, despite you being one of the most intelligent people in the room?
- ☐ **P**laying small, despite hating that feeling?
- ☐ **P**rocrastination, despite knowing the cost and stress of that?
- ☐ **P**ushing to exhaustion, despite having been burned out before?

- ☐ **S**elf-doubt, despite having a long list of skills and achievements to show for?
- ☐ **S**elf-hatred, despite longing to love yourself?

- ☐ **T**oo muchness, despite feeling already overwhelmed?
- ☐ **T**oo wired up to relax, despite doing yoga and meditating?

- ☐ Undervaluing your services/products, despite knowing the huge value they will bring your clients?
- ☐ Underselling your offers, despite knowing they are in the top quality range in the marketplace?
- ☐ Zero boundaries, despite knowing you need them desperately to protect your focus, energy, mood, and health?

How do you feel after going through this list? Are you mad at me for offering such a long list? Relieved you didn't resonate with many? Angry, shocked, ashamed… because you ticked off a lot of them?

If so, you're not alone. **Most successful women exhibit these self-sabotaging behaviors, myself included.** I was able to create this long ABC of Self-Sabotage™ because I know every single one of those patterns!!! Some I barely fall into, like gossiping and bitching, yet could I say I never exhibited those? Of course not. My top five - and I invite you to choose your top five too - were the following: fear of failure and fear of success (which creates a powerful, destructive double bind), people pleasing/approval seeking, and procrastination out of perfectionism.

If you feel frustrated after going through the list: great! **Your frustration is the important red flag your body is signaling you, and it is an invitation to dig deeper, find your blind spot, and "FLIP it!" to something wonderful!**

## Let's Understand Why We Sabotage Ourselves:

Our society believes business is based on the conscious design of products and services that solve a problem in the marketplace. Historically, until about three generations ago, business was in the hands solely of men. Men were indoctrinated by societal norms and expectations to be rational - "Strong boys never cry!" - and to focus on the numbers - "the language of business" - and their profits. Men were conforming to an artificial, inhumane ideal of 'fighters for success,' conditioned to push, push, push, and hustle, hustle, hustle, costing them their health, integrity, love, and family.

Women were historically taught to be 'emotional' and then judged for it, seen as 'hysterical'. This put women in a paradoxical situation when they entered the workforce in huge quantities after the last world wars and, in most countries, the 70s was when women were finally legally allowed to start their own businesses and borrow money from banks without needing a father's, husband's, or brother's signature.

The challenge was trifold: on the one hand, women were expected to behave like men in business because they entered a 'male playing field,' getting bombarded with men's rules and sportsmen play metaphors and war terminology as a business language.

On the other hand, they got messages like:

- "Don't be too male or you lose your femininity," keeping women stuck in the artificial stress of wardrobe choices that oscillated between military, dark grey suits with shoulder pads in the morning and slutty, glittering, skin-showing, curve-hugging body etuis at night.
- "Be aware of the other women, they want what you have!" installing deep mistrust leading to catfights among women at work, ensuring women would not follow the men's example of the 'good old boys' clubs' where all real business decisions were made over a glass of whiskey and a handshake at the bar or on the golf course.
- "You can't be both: a successful businesswoman AND a successful good mother and wife." triggering the permanent cycle of guilt and shame, dooming professional women to fail no matter how hard they tried in both areas of their lives, professionally AND privately.

And thirdly, the most recent development: women started to wake up to the fact that how business was run for many generations was not sustainable! Its exploitive nature, numbers obsession, and male illusion to be purely rational kill our climate, EVERYONE's health, relationships, and integrity. More and more women entrepreneurs say "no" to those outdated ways of running businesses and pour their heart, soul, and money into doing it **differently.**

Businesswomen are now on the search for new business models and new forms of leadership that are **sustainable, holistic, heart-centered, and soul-led, bringing and evolving men alongside them into the future!**

But the collective history is still stored as rules and habits in our subconscious mind. Combined with our personal life stories of early childhood traumas, loyalty patterns to our parents, and cultural demands on us women, **our subconscious mind is full of content that is not aligned with our conscious business goals and strategies and creates dangerous blind spots!**

As a Certified Master Neuroplastician - this is someone with trained expertise in applied neuroscience to help clients make lasting changes in their lives and at work - I can affirm that the male belief that men are the more rational gender and that business decisions are rational decisions is neuroscientifically proven to be wrong. **Our human brain doesn't make any decisions without feelings being involved!**

**Our actions are, mainly, subconsciously driven and not consciously designed!**

When our conscious mind and subconscious mind are in a conflict and want us to do opposing things - eat the full chocolate bar at 10 pm or not, buy one more online marketing training membership or not - **the subconscious mind always wins long term**!

## Examples:

### 1. The Perfectionist Procrastinator:

Sylvia, a coaching whiz, had the brilliant idea to launch a video content series showcasing her unique coaching process. She researched, trained, and planned consciously and meticulously. But every time she sat down to film, something held her back. The lighting wasn't perfect, the script needed tweaking, or her outfit wasn't 'professional' enough. Hours turned into days, then weeks, as Sylvia's perfectionism morphed into procrastination. By the time she finally overcame her self-doubt, the market had shifted, and the opportunity to be a trailblazer with this new method was lost.

**Blind spot:** Fear of failure and negative self-judgment disguised as a desire for perfection. This was combined with an old trauma from high school of humiliation caused by a photo of her on public display.

### 2. The Boardroom Freeze:

Emma, a seasoned executive, had aced every presentation throughout her career. However, during a crucial, all-men board meeting to secure a major investment, despite her consciously designed slides and rehearsed speech, her mind went blank. Her voice choked, her hands trembled, and she couldn't articulate her brilliant proposal. Shame washed over her, and the deal slipped through her fingers.

**Blind spot:** Loyalty to her father's rule that "girls have to be quiet when men talk" that she had associated with public speaking and the fear of being judged.

### 3. The Underachieving Trailblazer:

Diana, a former corporate powerhouse, dreamed of starting her own business and empowering other women entrepreneurs. She had the experience, the network, and even the support of renowned mentors. Yet, despite years of planning and countless courses, she remained paralyzed by self-doubt and insecurities, unable to take the first step.

**Blind spot:** Belief in being an 'imposter' and not deserving of success, rooted in unhealed emotional wounds from her early childhood.

*"Uncovering blindspots is not easy as long we ignore them.*
*Yet once we look for them with the right tool we can find and*
*flip them into something useful like pancakes in a pan!"*
—Sylvia Becker-H

## The Solution:

The following process is motivated by many, many tearful moments on my bedroom floor, being frustrated, and many sleepless nights worrying about my business. It is rooted in my over 35 years of research into human happiness and success principles, plus 27 years of working as a coach with thousands of clients. Which means it is tested. It works. It is neuroscience-based. I am now living proof of our 'FLIP powers.' I am now living an authentic, bliss-filled life with my New Zealand husband, Peter, for 24 years, two smart, kind sons, in a Spanish-style mansion on an old citrus orchard in Southern California. **I use the following process whenever I catch myself sabotaging my own efforts.** Can I guarantee that it will work for you too? No, we are all unique and our brains show a bigger range of neurodiversity than we all believed possible until just a few years ago. Yet, I invite you to test it. You have nothing to lose. Just pain and frustration. And a lot to gain. More freedom, more love, curation of your own identity, and more power.

# The FLIP it! Process™

**When to use it:**
Every time you feel frustrated about doing something or not doing something that you know is sabotaging your goals.

**Step 1: Stop Pushing and Analyzing.**
Quit what you normally do: analyzing and judging yourself. Instead, cultivate strong curiosity.

**Step 2: Deep Breath and Deep Drop.**
Use your breath to bring your attention inward, away from the external world, and drop into your body.

**Step 3: Ask and Sense.**
Ask yourself, "What is causing this pattern?" and wait for the answer to emerge as a sensation or message within your body and not as an analytical thought in your mind. The answer is revealing the blind spot!

**Step 4: Unearth and Release the Emotion.**
Identify the suppressed emotion underneath the blind spot. Allow yourself to feel it fully and release it. Now you are free from the past!

**Step 5: Make the FLIP.**
Choose what you want to feel, think, and do instead of the old sabotaging pattern.

**Step 6: Act on Your Choice.**
Take consistent action to solidify the new conscious behavior so that it turns into a new productive subconscious habit.

**Step 7: Celebrate it all.**
To overcome our brain's negativity bias we need to use conscious effort to celebrate every tiny proof of progress. That helps to hardwire our new choice of thinking, feeling, and acting. Celebration is the glue for sustainable self-directed change!

## Benefits:

- Increased self-awareness and emotional intelligence
- Reduced self-doubt and limiting beliefs
- Enhanced confidence and decisiveness
- Unlocking of your full potential for success and fulfillment

## Remember:

**You are not alone on this journey.** Many women entrepreneurs have fought and won the battle against self-sabotage. By employing the "FLIP it!" process, you can unlock your true power and transform your blind spots into stepping stones for extraordinary success.

Get started today and use your "inner pancake spatula power" to "FLIP it!" "It" being anything that pains you, frustrates you, or holds you back.

**Utilize the "FLIP it!" process daily and enjoy Becoming an Unstoppable Woman Entrepreneur who never stops evolving!**

## Nicole Curtis

She Rises Studios
Intl. Bestselling Author, Speaker, Crazy Chicken Lady

https://www.linkedin.com/in/nicole-curtis-sherisesstudios
https://www.facebook.com/nicolecurtiscrazychickenlady
https://www.instagram.com/nicolecurtiscrazychickenlady
https://www.sherisesstudios.com
https://www.facebook.com/groups/sherisesstudioscommunity

International Bestselling Author, Speaker and Crazy Chicken Lady. Nicole Curtis is a revered figure in women's leadership. With over 17 years of experience in personal growth and self-leadership development, Nicole is a sought-after expert.

As the co-creator of the celebrated Crazy Chicken Lady Merch line, prominently featured by She Rises Studios, Nicole exudes a unique blend of personality and empowerment. Her mission is to empower women to embrace growth, elevate their lives, and expand their horizons in both personal and professional aspects.

Through her engaging writing and compelling speeches, Nicole resonates with women worldwide, encouraging them to unlock their natural leadership potential and navigate life and business authentically. With her guidance, women are inspired to step into their true selves, leading with confidence and purpose on their journey towards self-discovery and success.

# SAY YES TO CLUCKIN' YOU!

By Nicole Curtis

In the world of entrepreneurship, where challenges abound and resilience is key, my transformative journey of becoming an unstoppable woman entrepreneur was initiated with a simple yet profound decision: "Say Yes To Being Me." This chapter embarks on an exploration of embracing authenticity and unleashing the unstoppable force residing within me as an aspiring entrepreneur. It dives into the profound insights, struggles, and triumphs I've experienced along this path, aiming to inspire and empower me to claim my own power and stand unapologetically in my truth.

To say yes to being you is to embrace your authenticity without reservation. It is a declaration that you have the freedom to do things your way, on your terms, and with unwavering confidence. Being unapologetically YOU can have a transformative impact on your entrepreneurial journey.

It is very important to not only acknowledge your worth but boldly stand up for yourself in the ever-evolving scenario of challenges, skeptical voices, and lingering doubts. Join me as I dive deeper into the different parts of asserting your value, establishing firm boundaries, and navigating the entrepreneurial world with amplified courage, resilience, and unyielding determination to help you navigate the entrepreneurial world bigger, braver, and bolder.

## Part 1: Unapologetically You

**Acknowledging your worth** is the key to confidently standing up for yourself in the face of challenges, doubters, and insecurities in the entrepreneurial world. This journey isn't just about knowing your value—it's about truly understanding it and using it as a strong foundation to navigate your path with resilience and confidence. It's about using your self-worth as a shield against doubts and as a tool to overcome obstacles.

At various points in my life, I've allowed the opinions and beliefs of others to influence how I see myself, leading to doubts about my abilities and worth. I used to believe these negative narratives, and as a result, I lacked self-respect and self-love. Learning to value yourself and acknowledge your worth isn't a simple task—it demands honesty and accountability. Recognizing your worth is a journey only you can embark on; it's your responsibility, not anyone else's.

At the core of embracing your authenticity and saying yes to being you lies the unwavering belief in **your capabilities**. This self-assertion is not a mere whisper; it's a powerful proclamation that resonates through every fiber of your being. It clearly declares that your ideas, talents, and contributions matter. They are not only valid, but they are indispensable to the narrative of your success. Armed with this mindset, you empower yourself not merely to navigate challenges but to rise above them, claiming your rightful space in the entrepreneurial world.

Your dreams, aspirations, and desires hold significant value, and you have the capability to attain them. You are inherently valuable, uniquely crafted, and hold innate potential. Embrace your authenticity and recognize that within you lies the power to manifest your aspirations. Your inherent qualities are your greatest strengths, serving as the foundation of your potential success. Do not hesitate to showcase your authenticity, for it is this genuineness that constitutes your superpower and embodies your inherent capabilities

The entrepreneurial journey can be an overwhelming rush, demanding significant portions of your time and energy. **Setting boundaries** is not just a strategic maneuver; it's an intentional act of self-care. In the sea of tasks and responsibilities, distinguish between the hustle that propels you forward and the burnout that threatens to extinguish your entrepreneurial flame. Ensure that your journey isn't just sustainable from a business perspective but also fulfilling on a deeply personal level. The act of setting boundaries becomes a self-love language, affirming your commitment to a journey that not only helps you thrive but also nourishes your well-being.

Ensuring enjoyment in all pursuits is vital. As my esteemed business mentor, Hanna Olivas, often emphasizes, "If you're not having fun, you're done," and she is right. While the demands of work are endless with tasks, projects, to-do lists, and deadlines, it is imperative to recognize that pleasure can coexist with productivity. Indeed, maintaining a positive state of mind is of utmost importance for me. Additionally, I integrate practices such as time blocking in my schedule or establishing boundaries—such as switching off electronic devices at a designated hour—to facilitate relaxation and rejuvenation. Acquiring skill in saying no also proves invaluable for me, ensuring that my time and energy are allocated wisely, thereby nurturing both my personal and professional well-being.

**Boldness.** It isn't just a luxury; it's an essential quality for entrepreneurial success. Embrace a bold attitude that not only navigates challenges but also turns them into opportunities. Instead of seeing setbacks as obstacles, view them as stepping stones toward your goals. Criticism, often seen as discouragement, can actually be an opportunity for constructive growth. Boldness isn't merely a strategic approach; it's a mindset that positions you as a fearless force, thriving rather than merely surviving.

**Imposter syndrome**. This is often a silent hurdle in the path to progress and loses its power when you acknowledge your intrinsic worth. Embrace your authenticity with unwavering resolve, standing confidently against the inner critic. The journey of entrepreneurship is undoubtedly challenging, but by recognizing and leveraging your inherent value, you fortify yourself against the crippling effects of imposter syndrome. It's not just about overcoming self-doubt; it's about rewriting the narrative and transforming self-doubt into a catalyst that propels you forward with renewed confidence.

**Failure**. Although often feared and avoided, failure is not a roadblock but a stepping stone to success. Rather than seeing failure as a defeat, view it as a valuable learning experience. Embrace the lessons it offers, using them to refine your strategies and turn setbacks into opportunities for growth. This perspective shifts setbacks into chances for profound development, guiding your entrepreneurial journey toward continuous evolution and success.

**Criticism**. This is a double-edged sword that can be discouraging or an opportunity for growth and becomes an art in resilient entrepreneurship. Handle criticism with grace, discernment, and an unwavering commitment to continuous improvement. Resilience is not a mere act of weathering the storm; it's about emerging from it stronger on the other side. By embodying resilience in the face of criticism, you transform challenges into opportunities for both personal and professional development.

**Self-acknowledgement**. In the relentless pursuit of success, celebrate your achievements, recognizing both the monumental victories and the subtle milestones. Self-acknowledgement allows for not just a positive mindset but also maintains a healthy work-life balance. By taking the time to celebrate victories, big and small, you fuel your momentum and reinforce your commitment to becoming an unstoppable woman entrepreneur. This journey is not just about reaching predetermined milestones; it's about acknowledging and relishing the progress made along the way, cultivating a mindset of gratitude and positivity.

**Asserting yourself**. Asserting yourself isn't equivalent to isolating yourself. Establishing a supportive network is crucial. Collaborate with individuals who share your vision, nurturing a community that promotes growth and mutual empowerment. Utilize collective strengths, celebrate achievements together, and tackle challenges with a unified spirit of resilience.

By acknowledging your worth and standing up for yourself in the entrepreneurial world with boldness, resilience, and an unwavering commitment to your authentic self, you pave the way for success. Saying yes to being you is a continuous process of growth, evolution, and unapologetic authenticity in this dynamic journey of self-discovery and empowerment. It's not just a mantra but a powerful declaration that echoes through every decision, action, and triumph, propelling you toward becoming an unstoppable force in the business world and beyond.

## Part 2: Be You in All Areas of Your Life

Being you extends beyond the confines of your business. This part explores the importance of authenticity in personal life, family, friendships, and community involvement as well as how it contributes to the holistic development of an unstoppable woman entrepreneur.

**Leading by example.** This is a multifaceted art that finds its roots in authentic self-leadership. This artistry extends beyond a simple surface-level demonstration; it explores the profound impact of authenticity on the very fabric of leadership qualities, decision-making processes, and the cultivation of a positive organizational culture. Authenticity serves as more than a buzzword; it's the foundational base upon which effective leadership is intricately built. This vibrant setting fosters an environment where genuineness and integrity become the guiding forces, intricately shaping every nuanced aspect of decision and action. Authentic self-leadership transcends simple imitation; it embodies values that nurture trust and transparency.

**The art of building authentic connections.** Communicating isn't just about exchanging pleasantries or swapping business cards; it's about forging genuine bonds that resonate from the heart. It's about being vulnerable, open, and sincere in your interactions, allowing others to see the real you beyond the surface level. Authentic connections are rooted in empathy, understanding, and mutual respect, creating a space where individuals feel heard, valued, and supported. It's about cultivating relationships that go beyond business transactions, where trust and transparency form the foundation for long-lasting partnerships. Building authentic connections means showing up authentically, embracing your true self, and creating meaningful connections based on genuine human connection rather than superficial appearances.

**Authentic marketing messages**. In an era inundated with a continuous overflow of marketing messages, authenticity emerges as a guiding light that not only sets you apart but also resonates deeply with your audience. They transcend the superficial; it's about adopting a genuine approach that not only builds trust but also creates a profound resonance with your audience on a deeper, emotional level. This resonation becomes the sturdy foundation of long-term business success, establishing an enduring connection with your target audience that transcends the temporary nature of mere transactions. Authenticity is the soul of your brand, a magnet that draws people toward a genuine and lasting connection.

Example: I absolutely love chickens, especially my 17 feathered friends :) For the longest time, I felt I needed to keep my love for chickens separate from business, thinking it wasn't relevant. However, embracing my authentic self and incorporating my passion for chickens into my marketing has been empowering. It's a reminder that authenticity is crucial in marketing. Embracing my true self and incorporating my passion for chickens into my messaging not only boosts my confidence and empowers me but also brings immense joy to others. It's not just about showing them who I am; it's about inviting them into my crazy chicken lady world. Knowing that it's putting a smile on their face warms my heart and brings a sense of connection that's truly special. So, I encourage you to embrace your true self in your messaging. Don't be afraid to share your passions and quirks with the world—they're what make you unique, unforgettable, and authentic.

**The offerings you present.** These gifts you share with the world are authentic reflections of your values and true self. Align your services and products with your authentic identity. Dive beneath the surface and explore how infusing authenticity into the core of what you offer enhances not only the quality of your offerings but also establishes a deep connection with your target audience that transcends mere transactions. Authenticity is not merely a marketing buzzword in this context; it serves as a guiding principle in the development of your products and services, guaranteeing that each creation is a genuine expression of your brand. In a competitive marketplace, authenticity acts as your distinctive trait, distinguishing you as an example of integrity in the eyes of your audience.

In essence, **authenticity** is not just a box for you to check; it's the golden thread that gracefully weaves through every facet of your professional journey. From the art of self-leadership and the intricate dance of building connections to the strategic details of marketing and the creative development of products and services, authenticity forms a cohesive and genuine narrative. It's not just a strategic maneuver; it is a way of being that resonates with others, builds trust, and moves you toward sustainable success. The authentic entrepreneur, like a bright star in the busy world of a crowded market, stands out, leaving an indelible mark not just in the business world but also in the lives of those they serve.

# Part 3: Establishing Business Principles

One of the pivotal and transformative milestones in my entrepreneurial journey unfolded when I consciously decided to establish a set of business principles. In this last part, I extend a guiding hand, leading you through the intricate process of creating your own principles.

**Business principles**. In essence, these serve as more than mere guidelines; they embody an unwavering guiding compass throughout the complicated twists and turns of your entrepreneurial journey. They represent the core values and beliefs of your business, offering clarity amidst the challenges of entrepreneurship. Think of them as your compass, guiding decision-making and keeping you aligned with your core values.

In both tough and successful times, company principles serve as a reference point for decision-making. They empower you to make principled choices and provide motivation to overcome obstacles.

**The process of crafting your business principles.** This is a foundational step for entrepreneurs at every stage of their journey, from those just starting out to seasoned professionals leading teams. It's a process that begins with self-reflection and introspection, regardless of where you are in your entrepreneurial path.

For those just starting out, crafting business principles is an opportunity to define your values and beliefs, shaping the foundation upon which your business will be built. It's about identifying what matters most to you personally and translating those values into actionable principles that guide your decision-making and behavior.

As your business grows and you begin to build a team, your business principles become even more critical. They serve as a compass, providing clarity and direction for both you and your team members. By clearly articulating your principles, you create a shared understanding of what your business stands for and how you operate, encouraging unity and alignment among team members.

Regardless of the stage of your entrepreneurial journey, it's essential to ensure that your business principles are aligned with your personal values. This alignment not only encourages authenticity but also strengthens your commitment to upholding these principles in every aspect of your business.

Adaptability is another crucial aspect of crafting business principles. As your business evolves, so too should your principles. Regularly review and reassess your principles to ensure they remain relevant and responsive to changing circumstances and market dynamics.

**Daily reflection.** This includes reading and following your business principles daily as a powerful practice that strengthens your commitment to being yourself in business.

Consistently revisiting these guiding principles cultivates a deeper connection with your values and beliefs, grounding you in a solid foundation as you navigate the complexities of business. This daily ritual serves as a reminder of your core ethos, empowering you to stay true to yourself and your vision amidst the myriad challenges and opportunities that arise in the business world.

The impact of this daily practice extends beyond simple reinforcement of your values; it influences every aspect of your mindset and decision-making process. Immersing yourself in your business principles regularly cultivates a heightened sense of self-awareness and clarity of purpose. This clarity becomes a guiding light, illuminating the path forward and enabling you to make decisions that are aligned with your values and long-term objectives.

This daily reflection on your business principles cultivates a mindset of growth and continuous improvement. As you internalize and apply these principles in your daily interactions and decision-making, you develop a habit of deliberate and intentional action. This proactive approach empowers you to identify areas for growth, seize opportunities for innovation, and navigate challenges with resilience and adaptability.

In essence, the transformative impact of reading and following your business principles daily lies in its ability to cultivate a strong sense of identity, purpose, and direction in your entrepreneurial journey. It serves as a core element of your personal and professional development, empowering you to lead with authenticity, integrity, and confidence as you strive for success and fulfillment in the dynamic world of business.

The journey of entrepreneurship is a profound and transformative one, filled with challenges, triumphs, and moments of self-discovery. As you navigate this ever-evolving adventure, remember how powerful authenticity, self-belief, and unwavering commitment to your values are. Saying yes to being ourselves, embracing our true essence, and infusing authenticity into every aspect of our entrepreneurial journey is not just a choice; it's a revolutionary act of self-love and empowerment. Let us continue to stand boldly in our truth, celebrate our unique gifts and contributions, and inspire others to do the same. Together, as unstoppable women entrepreneurs, we can create a world where authenticity reigns supreme, success is defined on our terms, and fulfillment knows no bounds. Say Yes To Cluckin' YOU!

XX Crazy Chicken Lady 🐣🐤👧

## Michèle Kline

President & Founder of Kline Hospitality Consulting

http://www.linkedin.com/in/michelekline
https://www.facebook.com/michele.kline
http://www.instagram.com/micheleklinekhc/
http://www.klinehospitality.com/

Argentinean immigrant Michèle Kline built a career in the Hospitality Industry "playing chess and not checkers".

In 2010, she founded "Kline Hospitality Consulting", where she enhances companies' culture and improves their operating procedures, with laser focus on leadership development. In 2018 she received the Learning & Development Professional of the Year award in her State.

As co-founder of "WTF! Walk the floors", a podcast focused on hospitality training, with a hint of wit she sheds light over the areas of opportunity leaders miss when managing from behind their desk. As a result, she was recognized within the Top 15 Hospitality Trainers internationally.

As a Certified Coach, Michèle also works with individuals 1:1 and in group settings. In 2022 she was selected as one of the Top 5 Coaches to look out for.

As part of her commitment to advocating for DEI&B, she co-founded "We THRIVE", a networking circle aimed to connect, empower, and transform Women.

# HOLD MY COSMO!

By Michèle Kline

I was in my early twenties and in charge of managing several departments within a few hotels, a large operation considering my age. One of my leaders, whom I grew to admire and appreciate with time, called me up one day and told me that my entire operation was grossly underperforming, making the company lose money. Without any time to react, the message was very clear to me that I was to take action immediately.

I wish I could tell you that I stayed quiet when he broke this news to me. But, on the contrary, my spicy Latin passion was all out, just like that, in a matter of seconds. Of course, I was not in a boastful mood when I received the call. Still, in all honesty, I used to run a very tight ship and was always looking for creative ways to stretch a tight budget and make it work while keeping hundreds of employees happy and the quality of service intact. I was, in many instances, making magic happen. And the company I worked for knew it.

At the time, my company did not have a robust platform to grant managers access to the "treasure box" where all the business' finance data was captured and displayed with the push of a button. Although we were responsible for managing millions of dollars with a blindfold, back then, for me to have a sort of view of where my operation was standing, I had to hunt people down for information or preferably "make friends." So, I decided to create a system unique to my operation which allowed me to know EXACTLY where I was standing with as much detail as possible.

Without hesitation, after my boss suggested that I was not performing, I pulled up my system and walked him through MY numbers. After a while of me showing my spicy Latin side (not a proud moment, I'm afraid) and proving to him that what he was alluding to was utterly inaccurate, I decided to offer him a solution to the company's problem. At that point, I felt even stronger about my numbers, and he was secretly convinced that I knew what I was doing. My solution… recover the loss! We both knew the loss was not in my region, although it was clearly impacting it. He didn't deny it. Win!

I knew then that I was up for a challenge. A BIG one. My operation was already running very slim, and there was truly no fat to carve from to recover such loss. But… I knew I could do it. I had a great team, and I could be very creative. So, I told my boss I would recover the loss. I told him I was going to make it happen. I told him to hold my Cosmo and watch me take this baby to that finish line.

For those of you unfamiliar with the expression "hold my beer," it is an expression joked about being said before someone does something dangerous without overthinking it. And because I am a girly girl, and Hollywood promoted Cosmopolitan to be a girly drink, that is the expression I use when I am about to embark on a dangerous journey.

This is a quick story that proves the importance of knowing our numbers. If I hadn't been as prepared as I was when I received that call, the outcome would have been dramatically different. I not only was able to prove that the loss had not been a result of my region, but I knew my numbers and my operation so well that I could recover the loss and make my region shine. Without skipping a beat.

Here's the secret sauce: you must have permanent conversations with your finances to know your numbers. This is how you make the right choices, stay on target, and become creative to stretch your budget to its fullest-both professionally and personally. Whether you run someone's operation or your own (and yes, this does include your household), here are some helpful tools to get you thinking. Enjoy the ride!

- **THE Date**. Schedule time in your calendar to work on finances weekly. Please get familiar with where the money is coming from and where it is going. This will allow you to make the necessary adjustments and fast. Be candid with yourself and keep your goals at the forefront, always!

- **Have a Budget**. Money goes as fast as it comes, and sometimes even faster. Having a budget will create stability and put you and your operation in a better position on a day-to-day basis and future. Budgeting also helps you keep your "eye on the prize" while working towards specific goals with a price tag. You can live a less stressful life when you know you have an emergency fund available, don't spend what you don't have, and are confident that you are planning for the future (i.e., retirement). Keep debt to a minimum. I was raised in a country where inflation and poor federal administration were common, "textbook" recessions every ten years were the norm, and loans were tough to obtain. This taught me that you buy what you need and save for what you want. I'm not saying to deny yourself from dreaming about investing in something you cannot afford. What I am suggesting is for you to get organized and create a plan to lead you there. But, by no means, get into meaningless debt that will cause unnecessary stress.

- **Risk vs Reward**. Before making an important financial decision, measure the risk behind that decision and the repercussions that you may have. Then, ask yourself if the reward is greater than the risk. Only then, act.

- **Finances & Self-care**. Put your financial house in order as part of your self-care routine. As Women, we tend to invest most of our time in others. Perhaps an employer because we feel we must prove ourselves. Maybe our Family because we feel the responsibility for their care. In many instances, both scenarios apply. But eventually, life throws a curveball at us, and we are found in a tough spot. So, taking care of your finances is crucial and should be considered a large part of self-care.

- **Your Worth**. Lastly, and this one's for you, knowing your worth is extremely important. Start by compartmentalizing your thoughts, feelings, and emotions. This psychological mechanism is beneficial when asking for a pay increase, preparing a proposal, spending money on yourself, and the list goes on. Do all the things you tend to do for others, for yourself. Once you can separate these, you will start thinking straight and understanding your worth.

Every decision we make has an impact of some sort. By becoming financially savvy, you will be able to make more educated decisions, which will positively impact your personal growth, the operation you run, and ultimately, your bottom line. This way, when life throws a curveball at you, you can say, "Hold my Cosmo!"

## Sarah Thayer

Co-founder of Mama Knows Money

https://www.linkedin.com/in/sarah-thayer
https://www.facebook.com/sarah.naomi.thayer
https://www.instagram.com/sarah.naomi.thayer/
https://linktr.ee/_sarah_thayer

Sarah Thayer was born and raised in a self-employed family and grew up working in her family's businesses. She understands the joys and challenges of working for yourself. After college, she worked in human services, retail and banking, searching for her passion in life. She loved helping people but never truly felt she was making a difference. In 2015, Sarah and her husband, Owen, had their daughter and the pull of her heart to make more of a difference was stronger than ever. Evanora's amazing spirit inspires her every day and is the reason Sarah took a leap of faith to help families achieve their goals and dreams through financial empowerment. She left her banking career of 10 years to start helping families and businesses discover how money works. Sarah is thankful every day for the changes she sees in her client's lives and the impact on their futures.

# MONEY MINDSET

By Sarah Thayer

There is so much I could say about our thoughts, feelings, and emotions when it comes to money, but I'm going to keep it short and sweet. Money affects every aspect of our lives. How we think about money, whether positive or negative, influences our relationship with it.

When we first start in the world, our parents are our foundation for all things. They teach us how to throw a ball, deal with our emotions, cook, clean, and so much more. If you have children, you may find yourself teaching those same life lessons to them. We learn so much from our parents, consciously or unconsciously, including our money habits. If you're like most people, myself included, you probably grew up in a home where money wasn't a regular topic of conversation. In most homes, when we talk about money, it tends to be negative or not discussed. My question is, why?

We have been told history repeats itself. Chances are your money habits are similar to your parents', and your grandparents' money habits are similar to their parents'. So if history repeats itself, what do you think your children's money habits will be? That answer is definite; I want my girl to have more. If you don't have children, think about the impact you want to have on those around you. Do you want to give more? Be the person in your family who can help when needed without hesitation. If you have a positive relationship with money and you have developed healthy money habits, you have built a strong foundation to grow your money mindset. I hope to share little tips and tricks to help take it to the next level.

So, first thing, and in my opinion the most important: money is a tool. Yes, read that again. Money is a tool. It's a thing we use to accomplish something. Let's start looking at money as a way to accomplish goals and dreams instead of defining what we can and can't do. This might be the hardest concept, but when you start looking at money as a tool, it changes your thought process. Think about it this way, our phones do a lot for us, but we aren't letting them tell us what we can and can't do. We aren't checking our phones to see if we can travel or not. We may use them to decide where we want to go and how we will get there, but not if we can. Now, use money like we use our phones. Not tell us if we can go, but as a tool to decide where we want to go and how we will get there.

As you are reading this, you may think, "This all sounds awesome, but I don't have enough money." Well, remember, money is a tool. For example, If we were offered a position with a company that required us to wear a suit every day and we only had one suit, we would be running out to get more suits. Money is the same way; if we don't have enough, we must figure out how to get more. It could mean finding a career that pays more than what we earn now. It could mean reevaluating our monthly budget and cutting out unnecessary expenses. Perhaps it means starting our own business or side hustle. When you think about money as a tool, you become more creative and inspired to find ways to meet your goals.

I think it's important to touch quickly on needs versus wants or unnecessary expenses. Needs are our necessities, such as food, water, and shelter, or help us to survive. Wants are something we desire and don't need to survive - for example, a designer bag. I want a designer handbag anytime I am out shopping. I may even convince myself I cannot survive without it, but at the end of the day, that bag is not paying my mortgage or putting me closer to my goals. It's a tough conversation to have, but one that is needed. Look where you are spending your money and evaluate if your expenses are wants or needs. "Don't tell me where your priorities are. Show me where you spend your money and I'll tell you what they are." – James W. Frick.

As we start to see money as a tool, it will change how we think and feel about money. Affirmations are essential to encourage this new relationship with money and continue to grow our money mindset. If you aren't familiar with affirmations, they are positive statements you say or write to yourself daily. Why would we say money affirmations to ourselves? Because they will encourage us to continue to think positively about money. At first, it will seem strange and weird, but just like exercising is uncomfortable when you start, as the process becomes easier and more natural. So what are a few money affirmations we can say to ourselves?

- Money is a tool to help me accomplish my goals and dreams.
- I have a healthy relationship with money.
- Money allows me to have more time and freedom.
- I am smart and make good money decisions.
- Money helps me to change the lives of those around me.

These are just a few you can use or write your own that align with your beliefs and goals. Work on saying or writing these daily. One of my favorite ways to remember to say my affirmations is to write them on an index card and hang them on my bathroom mirror. I am reminded to say them as soon as I wake up and start the day with a positive mindset.

One of my favorite affirmations is "Money helps me to change the lives of those around me." You have to define what that means to you. Does it mean teaching your children healthy money habits they can pass on? Is it creating generational wealth for your children, their children, and then their children? Is it being the go-to person for your family when there is an emergency or need? Is it providing funding to organizations, giving back to the community, or changing the world? Stop for a moment and think about this. How could money help those around you?

When you are wondering if this mindset change is worth it or if you can do it, look back at what you wrote and keep going.

I believe one of the most significant changes we can make in our lives and those around us is generational wealth. I see generational wealth as creating strong, healthy money habits that will change our lives, our children's lives, their children's lives, and so on. I believe that through this process, we will create inheritable wealth that will allow us to leave a legacy for our children. We can accomplish so much with just a few adjustments to our thinking.

Paying yourself first is an important, often overlooked positive money habit for generational wealth. This is probably one of the last things we tend to do with our money. We pay our mortgage, utility bills, credit cards, etc., but when do we pay ourselves? You are the most critical expense that you should be paying, but I would argue the long overdue, final notice bill you don't want to deal with. There are so many other monthly expenses and bills; how can you afford to set a little aside for yourself? Well, I am sure we have heard this in other aspects of our lives, and our money health is not any different; make yourself a priority. Yes, make yourself a priority.

As women, we tend to think of ourselves last. I heard many years ago a saying that made me stop and think. I don't know who said it, but that doesn't make it any less powerful. "Fill up your cup because you can't pour from an empty cup." Apply this to money. If saving for yourself is not a priority now, whose priority will you be when you are older? Think about your future and what you want after your children are grown and you have retired. Do you want to travel? Do you want to help care for your grandchildren? Do you want the freedom to do what you want? Changing your thoughts and money mindset allows you to put yourself first when saving.

Wow, I don't know how, but we have reached the end of the chapter. I hope my passion for creating a positive money mindset has inspired you to feel and think differently about money as well as spark a change. I am blessed and thankful to be able to share this with you.

## Priya Ali Richards

Energi Living 365 Wellness Group
CEO/Master Coach/Energy Empress/Intuitive

http://www.linkedin.com/in/priya-ali-3237487
http://www.facebook.com/priyaali
http://www.instagram.com/startliving365
https://energimagazine.love/?fbclid=IwAR0PegT0yCE8GxPjTUYv2
NWnk16i5eDwFWW_3zX-nZdOaWWNIrDQwK6KrFE

Priya Ali, a dedicated entrepreneur, is a wife and mother of four children, and four fur babies. She has led a successful personal and executive coaching practice, Energi Living 365, since 2007. After dropping out of high school at the age of 17, she quickly developed her entrepreneurial skills and never looked back. Energi Living 365 is dedicated to enabling dramatic personal and professional growth amongst its clients. Through highly personalized coaching and guidance, Energi Living 365 empowers clients to establish positive, productive thought processes and behaviours. Priya also possesses unique intuitive abilities as a third-generation intuitive healer and medium that she applies in each of her service offerings. This intuitive capacity allows her to quickly extract valuable insights from individuals and social groups, providing clients with guidance that is both objective and keenly insightful. Priya Ali has cultivated her natural talent through a wide range of professional certifications and accreditation to maximize her capacity to support the personal, professional, spiritual and physical goals of her clients.

# HOW DOES IT FEEL TO BE A MILLIONAIRE?

By Priya Ali Richards

One day I was out for lunch with a friend. We were reviewing our professional successes and he asked me, "How does it feel to be a millionaire?" I was so taken aback. What was he even talking about? I'm not a millionaire. I just smiled and said, "Yeah, it's great."

As a single mompreneur, I never had a steady paycheck. I always used to stress at the first and fifteenth of the month, as a big chunk of money would be due for bills. I would have that big chunk of money, but I feared a time would come when I didn't. As a result, I would often pay my bills late after I secured the next big chunk of money. It was a vicious cycle that kept me anxious and disempowered, both of which contradicted what I was teaching and preaching. I was living a very comfortable lifestyle, but in some ways, I didn't feel it belonged to me, nor did I feel I belonged to it.

Shortly after, I was in the park with my four dogs, Kingsley, Duchess, and the pups they had recently. All of a sudden, a very attractive city rep approached us, stating there was a complaint that we were allowing our four Maltese to run off-leash. After turning on my best charm, he said he would let us go without a ticket, which would be $200. I said ok, and went home. About a week later, I returned home from my aunt's virtual funeral. The doorbell rang, and it was the attractive city rep. He came to tell me that when he checked into it, I didn't have up-to-date licenses for them and I needed to pay those fees. I told him the timing was very bad and that I had just come from a funeral. He said that he would give me a couple of weeks to remit the payment.

Two weeks later, our handsome city rep returned, and I had yet to pay the bill. When I opened the door, I could tell the friendly flirtation vibe was over and replaced by a "you didn't keep your word, and I'm mad" vibe. I found myself trying to plead out of paying the fees, and then he gave me the ticket and said, "You have to pay both the ticket and the fees." I started crying, explaining I was supporting a family of 6 on my own and that cash was tight. He said he was sorry and left.

As I closed the door behind him, I wiped my tears, and then I caught myself. I caught myself in my own lie. I had enough money to pay those dog fees when he asked the first time. I had enough money to pay them now and for the ticket. I had just been so used to telling my single mom sob story. I realized I was telling my old story, and that story was keeping me out of what my new, true story was. Each of us has a money story. We tell a story about our financial situation: some of us have multiple stories, a story for ourselves, a story we tell our friends or family, and a story we tell strangers. Some of the stories are true: and some are not. Some are the money stories we inherited from our parents or absorbed from the news.

I grew up in a money story that said we did not have money, and we would tell people we did not have money. About six months ago, I ran into a classmate from elementary school, and we were reminiscing about our childhood and neighborhood. She said that I lived in an affluent neighborhood and that she lived in a low-income neighborhood. I was stunned. How could that be? My parents were always saying that we had no money. When I questioned my mother about this shortly after, she said, "Well, we had the money for the important things, but we weren't super rich." The essential things she was referring to were our upscale home, above-average vehicle, frequent trips, and our cottage. We didn't have name-brand snacks or clothing and had homemade snacks for school and even some dreadful homemade clothing. We weren't rich enough for my parents to feel abundant, and if anyone had more money than they did, they not only felt they were not rich, they felt they were poor.

I saw how their story contributed to my story, but I had taken over and gone to the next level. Not only did I not acknowledge my abundance, but I also chose to hide it because I had experienced situations where people wanted me or interacted with me for my money. So, somewhere along the line, I created the untrue story of not having money so I wouldn't be or feel like I was being taken advantage of for my money. I performed all the exercises, clearings, and reprogramming for myself that I offer my clients seeking to create abundance and wealth. Finally, I decided and declared that I was ready to let go of that old story and step into my new one. I went straight to my computer and paid those dog licensing fees. Our attractive city rep was instantly notified, and about an hour later, he phoned to say that he would rip the ticket up since he had not filed it in the system yet and the fees were paid.

Over the next few days, I went through my finances with a fine tooth comb. As I said earlier, one of the things that would stress me out the most was having chunks of cash come out twice a month when bills were due. To create ease, I calculated the average amount of my variable bills. I then took those amounts and broke them down to a daily cost. I took my fixed expenses and did the same, and then set up automatic daily payments for each to be withdrawn and paid from my checking account. Having the smaller amounts come out daily not only allowed me to have a more consistent cash flow, it gave me the peace of mind that my bills were always paid and paid on time. This method also allowed me to eliminate a loan that I had, by breaking the payments down into daily amounts. This really shifted my mindset on bill payments, and I held the perspective that I was paying daily for what I used. I acknowledged how appreciative I feel to have access to all those wonderful things like hydro, water, heat, and internet. I got so excited seeing those amounts go out each day. I'm not sure the utility companies shared my excitement with all those payments, but everything was always on time.

When I reviewed my financial situation both on my own and with my financial advisor, I was quite shocked. The story I was seeing was vastly different from the one I was telling. I saw before my very eyes what my friend had seen before. I sat in my office staring at those numbers and then asked myself, "How does it feel to be a millionaire?" It was then that I saw that the efforts I had been putting in all those years, the dedication, the laying of the groundwork, and the perseverance had paid off, and I didn't even know it. I restructured my business plan and reduced my work week, began to travel more, and hit my best year in revenues earned. I have continued my daily bill payment method and even expanded it to help me make smart purchases and declutter my home. I check how many years I have had something along with how much I paid for it. For example, I bought a dining set in 2006 for $1300 that I finally gifted to someone this year. $1300, divided by the 16 years I had the table, comes out to $81.25 per year, which breaks down to $0.22 per day. Nearly 15,000 meals were eaten by my family at that table, not to mention the number of parties, family meetings, crafts, and homework that it served us for. Seeing this allowed me to feel satisfied that I had gotten my money's worth out of it and feel good about letting it go.

Raising my awareness around my money story and doing the work to bring all of me into a place aligned with my desired money story was life-changing. By breaking things down into a daily cost, I have successfully eliminated debts, taken the stress out of bill payments, and become more aware of the cost of living the life I desire. Realizing I was a millionaire didn't change my life in any way. I still invest and spend the way I did before knowing so. What did change my life was letting go of the story that I was a struggling single mompreneur because it allowed me to be more, and in being more, that allowed me to become more, and becoming more allowed me to offer more to others. I love that I am the same person either way, but embodying my truth created an opportunity to feel like a million bucks every day.

## Ashley Pakulski

The Mompreneur Coach:
Empowering Moms for Visibility and Success

https://www.facebook.com/groups/mompreneurssuccesscircle/
www.instagram.com/theashleypakulski
https://linktr.ee/TheMompreneurCoach

Introducing Ashley Pakulski, The Mompreneur Coach— Specializing visibility & success for Mompreneurs. Dedicated to empowering Moms to overcome self-doubt, show up confidently, and attract dream clients with her Signature Framework.

As a single mom, Ashley understands the challenges mothers face firsthand. Embracing her own journey, she offers a transformative approach tailored for Mompreneurs striving to thrive in both business and life.

As your trusted guide, Ashley will help you tap into your potential, step into confidence, and achieve your next level of success.

# UNSTOPPABLE FORCE

By Ashley Pakulski

You have that feeling within yourself that you know deep down that there is something greater out there for you. You have a vision for your business, and you know the legacy you want to leave behind. Entrepreneurship can be a hard and lonely road if you let it be and make it that way for yourself. Running a business is not only about how to run it but about learning to overcome the battles you have been fighting within that you need to release and let go of to step into your most powerful and higher version of self. We all have things we need to work through that we consciously and subconsciously know we need to heal. Success is 80% mindset and 20% strategy but I'm no mathematician. However, a certain percentage needs to be added as it is also the tribe you surround yourself with. How many times do you feel you are on top of the world, and then in the next moment you find yourself trying to pick yourself up off of the ground trying to get yourself back up?

Entrepreneurship is a roller coaster ride. Everything I am sharing with you right now you are either going through or will soon. You will be on cloud nine and then you will feel like giving up. You will have times you want to throw in the towel and call it quits! I'm not saying this to disappoint you BUT instead to show you that it won't and doesn't have to be hard because you have the tools to help you alongside your journey. So, when times do get tough, you will know how to listen to yourself, take a step back, and keep investing every day into doing the inner and mindset work instead of ignoring it and then self-sabotaging yourself.

Let me share with you my journey. I experienced trauma and addiction in my life, and it affected me and my family dearly. I made peace with it now, and I trust that with everything I have been through, God knows his plan for me. I know deep down that I am made for something more. I know my story is meant to help people worldwide. We all have a story to help other people, and it is up to us to take our message and make the world a better place.

I know we may be in different spots of our journey, but it doesn't matter if you are a new or seasoned entrepreneur. These tools and strategies are designed to help you and fuel you. Just like a car needs gas, you need to fuel yourself. There was a time I was in a really dark place, and I took myself out of that dark place and saw the light, but let me tell you, just like your entrepreneurial journey being a roller coaster, this was an up-and-down road for me too. I was trying to find myself and heal wounds that I never imagined actually affected my day-to-day actions, aiming to show up as my authentic self. I did the work but was still being blocked and not able to move forward. Yes, I made several accomplishments even my business today I am not where I want to be but I am further along than where I used to be. You need to remember that too. Where you were five years ago you were praying you have now. It's being in the moment and being your higher version self now. It's when you work through your limiting beliefs you get different results.

Trust me, I am doing the work, and I think I am over it - little do I know it smacks me in my face again, all resurfaced and ready for me to go deeper and work through it. Just like a good friend of mine said, " Sometimes we think we work through something but we only touch the surface. When God knows we are ready to fully work through it, it pops up." Let me tell you, it smacks you right in your face. But it isn't made to turn you down and break. It's meant to happen so you can reach that next level. You need to break those walls down and step into the new foundation. Doing the work isn't you waving a wand and fixing it - it will continue for the rest of your life. 10k a month Ashley will need to show up differently and step into another, higher version self, becoming the 100k a month Ashley. Each level is going to dig deeper and do the work.

Let's look at this example. You have a platter of gold strategy to bring in three million dollars within the year. Two coaches do the same work step-by-step. Coach A is signing on clients consistently and easily, and Coach B is struggling and getting frustrated, not being able to sign on clients. The strategies are the same, but what is getting in the way? It's easy to blame the program, isn't it? It's YOUR LIMITING BELIEFS; your thoughts, feelings, and actions. How you believe and view things. Trust me, I get like this at times too. I feel tense and get frustrated, but that's when I need to take my hand off the wheel, surrender, and go through my toolkit. Somewhere, my limiting belief can be showing up and blocking me from my success. Now, I'm the type of person who can give the best advice to others, but when it comes to me, I tend to take the lesson longer, but again, that's a belief. It's about stepping into your power.

We all have doubts and insecurities - no person on this planet doesn't have that. But it's what happens when we do the work and what is on the other side of it all. That is why it is key to have your tribe of women. Stop playing small. Do the things that are going to stretch you, that you know are going to make a difference in your business, alongside the inner and mindset work. You are going to move mountains. You are capable and worthy of everything you desire. Somewhere down the line, you may not be feeling it, and it leads back to childhood wounds. You may think it's not affecting you and is blocking you from your success.

Let me share another example with you in real-time. I will openly admit I take things too personally and I make assumptions at times. This comes from the person who drank a lot to numb her pain and forget things. This came from wounds I had since a child from abuse, not being heard, and bullying which all affected my confidence and my identity, and my self-esteem was low. Now, when I was digging deeper into this, I was like, "What if I have low self-esteem? No, I don't." But, when I dug deeper and started to become aware of what triggered me and my emotions and started questioning where this feeling was coming from, that is when I realized, " Oh man, this links back to my past of not feeling worthy." Yes, I had the proof of my being mistreated and what was said to me, but that's it. I took people's lies and made them believe that I was unworthy of anything. So, my brain found evidence when things didn't work for me if someone commented something or if I didn't sign on a client I was unworthy of it. The best is when I was about to sign clients and they backed out, or if I was working towards something and then all was going well but at the last minute it was about to fall apart, but then worked out in the end.

The belief I have is that something is bound to go wrong before it gets better. It's things like that that you need to start working through and become aware of. Whatever you tell your brain, it will find proof as to why it's not working or won't. That's why it's easier to look at the proof of what's going on in the economy and say it is bad, people fail, it's a scam, etc. It's safer to say and agree with it. How your inner is is exactly how your outer is. Sometimes, people say all is going well, and out of nowhere, something happens. I always like to question and ask, "What were you thinking and feeling before that?"

This is going to bring you to one of the first steps of my signature framework. This has three pillars including:

1. **Mindset Mastery 101:** Transform Your Thoughts, Transform Your Life.
2. **Routines & Habits for Success:** Building Your Roadmap for Success.
3. **Dream Client Blueprint:** Your Roadmap to Client Attraction Success.

I will share bits of it to help you along your journey running your business and living the life you desire.

## AWARENESS:

The first step to any change, including the next level you want to hit in your business, is that you need to be aware. You have to become aware of your FEELINGS, THOUGHTS, and ACTIONS. A lot of times we can push our emotions to the side numbing them with food, shopping, alcohol, and pure avoidance. When we start becoming aware and questioning our thoughts, feelings, and actions, we are able to heal. If you want to change, you have to do something different. Our day-to-day is run by our subconscious mind 95% of the time; this goes way beyond our conscious awareness. When you learn to rewire your subconscious mind, you will reach the next level of success. Awareness helps manage your emotions and rewire your brain. Your subconscious is always working and absorbing everything - that's how your beliefs are formed. To become more aware you can practice meditation, observe your thoughts and reactions, and journal.

Remember, you can't control other people, but you can control yourself. Start becoming attuned to your thoughts, feelings, and actions. Take out a journal and take some deep breaths. Start free writing the thoughts you have about yourself, your business, and your life. Start becoming aware of where these come from and start replacing them with truths. I always call limiting beliefs your little lies because they are just that. This brings me to the next step.

## REPROGRAMING THE SUBCONSCIOUS MIND:

You are hearing me talk about your subconscious mind, and this is so important and key for you to understand to break through anything in your life, create those new habits, and achieve the life you desire. There is so much that goes into this, and from reading my chapter, if there is one thing that you can walk away with, this is what I want you to remember. I'm sure you know about this, but a lot of times we are AWARE and we KNOW, but our mind and body are out of sync, including our emotions. Now, I'm not the guru in this, but I do have my own fair share of things I have learned and studied over the years from what I have learned and things I practiced myself. Of course, there is also what I have seen from raising my little human and her taking all this in as she faces her challenges - she is a resilient little girl. So when I hear people say kids are kids, they don't understand that is wrong. This is the best time, and at a young age as they are, babies teach themselves these things. This is when your beliefs about the world are stored because, from a young age, they say even in your mom's womb when she is pregnant with you until the age of seven, you are creating your initial impressions of the world.

Now, let's go back to your first step. It was for you to write out all your beliefs and become aware of your thoughts, feelings, and actions. When you write them out, you can look back to when these beliefs were formed, why you are doing the things you are doing, and really tune in. Be gentle. Trust me, a lot of times people think they are lazy or procrastinating, but doing the inner and mindset work and healing yourself can get VERY exhausting - you feel like you don't want to do anything. Your body is healing and it's ok to feel it out. I truly believe it's at this time that the shift is happening within, and you just go with it.

But back to the topic of what we are talking about. Now you are aware and it's all about reprograming your subconscious mind. There are many ways you can do this, and you have to find what works best for you. I feel I am best suited to the old-fashioned way of repetition, believing the evidence, and showing it to your brain. The more your brain sees it, the more it believes it, and this can start with something small. I will talk about the things I do more in-depth ahead as it is part of what I do daily, and this is key to your growth. I don't want to fully give it away now, but it includes breathwork, meditation, affirmations, journaling, and being present while practicing mindfulness.

See, our brain is designed to keep us safe. We can believe what we set out to believe. In the earlier gold platter strategy, one coach (Coach A) is killing it, making sales, and signing on clients so easily and consistently. Coach B is struggling. I have been that coach for years, and it's not that I don't know what to do. I know very much what to do. I have invested in myself, worked with coaches, and learned from the best. But it was ME. I had to get over it, and many times I thought I worked through things, but I was self-sabotaging myself, and that is why at any level you reach in your business, at each level, you will need to dig deep and do the inner and mindset work.

It is you who gets in your own way. You think you are good, but the excuses you tell yourself that you can't do something or that it's the economy are not that. It's your brain protecting you. It's FEAR. So once you become AWARE and start using these tools to help you reprogram your subconscious mind, you will start to see different results.

One thing I mentioned before and that I want to share here is that our mind consciously knows everything that we want but becomes aware of our body how it is feeling and our emotions. We may think positively, but how much do you truly believe? This is the key part. I meet people daily who talk about this but FULLY DON'T BELIEVE. When you believe, you don't need proof or to be realistic because anything can happen, and once you tap into that, the possibilities are endless. It's like someone playing the lottery - they want to win, but deep down, they think it is a scam they won't win. They will block themselves not just from winning but from so much more. Trust me, I have been in situations I had no idea how I would get out of, and with that belief and surrendering, it all worked out. Things LEGIT fell into my lap. It's not luck. It's the fact there is a Higher Power out there, and I believe in God. He helps when you surrender. It's the belief. So yes, it's reprogramming your subconscious mind, but it all links. That's what it truly is - the BELIEF. If you can understand this, you will move mountains.

Let's look at another example from my life. I truly believe in God. I had people always say you can't just dream, you have to take action, and yes, that's true. We all have our journeys, and some people get it fast and some slow. You hear about the overnight success. It's the journey, the work you do on yourself. I have faith and I believe my dreams are working out in my favor, and if something doesn't go out as planned, I know if it's not this, it is something better. I don't force my actions; I don't burn myself out. All it takes is that one step and action and BAM, everything sets.

I have days that I have no clue what I am doing but I tap into my visualization, prayer, breathwork, and meditation and take that inspired action. When I start to feel the pressure, I take a step back. I surrender and I say, "God, right now I am feeling the pressure. I surrender it all to you, can you lead me the way? I'm taking a step back. I am going to go do something fun, walk my dog, whatever!" I go about my day. and guess what? I come back and BAM, it works out. So that's the belief. Don't say affirmations if you don't believe them. Always say the next thing that is believable. This takes work, but it's fun. You are on your own path and your own time. This isn't a race or about who is better. If you will keep resisting and pushing, you will only slow yourself down.

Listen to your intuition. I am so much further ahead than I was five years ago, and that's the same for you. When you remove the guilt and shame, you are an unstoppable force. God moves mountains for you.

Opportunities come. But you have to believe in yourself. Feeling is the key too. Feeling as if you already have it.

Here is another example. Do you find yourself saying it's hard to find clients? Your program isn't working, this business is too saturated? You are having beliefs resurface, yes, but also, when you think that you are blocking yourself from success because you are doubting and you are in lack, what happens is your brain will find proof, and BAM, you are right - you can't do this! So what do you do? You quit or feel stuck, and it's the same rabbit hole. When you shift your energy, use affirmations, and reprogram your subconscious mind, you learn to love what you do...opportunities happen, things begin to shift, and change and clients come to you. Money comes to you unexpectedly and this is a fact. Why? Because it happens to me on a daily basis when I know things aren't working out the way I want them to or I am forced to go back to step one and work through the steps.

So it's not woohoo or a fluke. It's because I truly believe. I don't care about facts and research. I care about how I am feeling, and I know if I want something, if God wants it for me, it will happen, but you have to ASK, BELIEVE, RECIEVE. My favorite quote in the Bible is MATTHEW 7:7 "Ask and it will be given to you; Seek and you will find; Knock and the door will be opened to you." Let's go into the next part of my Signature Framework.

## ROUTINES & HABITS FOR SUCCESS:

This is the key. Mindset and inner work are the groundwork. As I said, you can have all the strategies in the world, but when you have your inner critics blocking you from taking the action you know you need to be taking, then that is what makes you self-sabotage. This is your fuel. Do you have a morning routine? This is so key to your success. I remember when I first started doing this on my healing journey. I thought I invented something until I searched online and saw that multi-millionaires were doing the same thing. Oprah shares her morning routine religiously, and it's a must for her. It's true - how you start your day, you end your day. If you don't have a morning routine, I highly recommend you start for at least five minutes a day and increase or start with one thing. This helps instill better habits. This helps boost your confidence in yourself and helps regulate your nervous system and be in the present moment. What can you include now?

- Prayer
- -Meditation/Breathwork
- -Personal Development
- -Journaling
- -Healthy Meal/ Supplements
- -Affirmations
- -Workout

We can have it all, and it's doing things like this that fuels you up and ignites your growth. If you feel you don't have enough time in your day, it's time to get up at 4/5 am. When the world is sleeping, you are up getting ready and taking on the day. You get so much done. You are in the driver's seat of your day. Be gentle with yourself too! Habits take a while to break and implement, so if you skip something or fall off the wagon, give yourself the grace to focus on the good you are accomplishing. You can do it. Just find easier ways to help you through it. It's only hard in your mind if you make it hard. If you slip off, it's ok. It can take you six months to do it as long as you are taking those baby steps.

Those small steps are what lead to greater results. TRUST ME. It is that 1% a day you do that adds up to your transformation. I read that 1% is 365% at the end of the year. This leads me to the last part of my Signature Framework.

## ATTRACT YOUR DREAM CLIENTS/ATTRACT YOUR DREAM LIFE:

This is the part that starts in the mind but is the fun, creative work you do daily to get what you want. Now, this can come sooner than expected, but a lot of times we get in our own way. How are you self-sabotaging yourself with getting your dream clients coming to you or living the dream life you desire? Look back into your life and remember the things you wanted to achieve or wrote about, and now have them. Look at the times you said, "I am going to hit this goal," and you did it. You have the passion and desire for your business and to create the life you desire for your family and yourself. You have the drive and fire within you. You are taking action, and then, somewhere down the road, you start becoming busier, you are overwhelmed, you are forcing signing clients on, and your energy is scarce. Trust me, I was there.

I want to share something with you. I hated sales and becoming an entrepreneur. What do we do? We sell. I had to go back to step one and work through my beliefs around selling, where they came from, and also, my confidence. Deep down, I was carrying deep-rooted beliefs that I was not worthy enough because, subconsciously, I stored everyone's lies about me. Which, in reality, are what they are feeling within themselves. People know when you have something greater within you; they will pull you down because when you succeed, and you do all the good you want to achieve in life, they will have no choice but to look at their fears right in the face. So, what is the easiest thing to do is to sit in the same place, and even better, find your people to stay in the same place. But trust me, when you find your tribe and you trust yourself, you know you are worthy. BUT the actions you take on a day-to-day basis are because of these beliefs, and they show up in your business and your life.

You need a plan, but you don't need to fully know how. Have a strategy you can create for your business that you can use rinse and repeat. Where are your ideal clients and who is your dream client? Know her and speak to her to bring her to you. When your mind is clear, you will attract the right people to you. I know when I am under pressure, I attract comments from trolls, but when I am fueled up to believe in myself, that's when I am attracting the right people to me. I know I am working through this still, but I have seen many shifts and examples so what I am saying is true.

In the end, you have received gold here. You have many stories that you can take and put the missing pieces to your puzzle on your entrepreneurial journey. There is an unstoppable force around you guiding you. You have to trust in it and surrender. Watch everything flow together. What do you need to release and let go of right now to move forward in your life? What is blocking you from taking that next step; no, it's not because you are stuck or don't have time. You are getting in your own way, and it's time to step in your TRUE power.

Focus on what you need to be doing more of and start doing it. Start showing up confidently and authentically YOU. I always say, ask yourself what you need to do right now to get to where you need to be, or most importantly, be your higher version self and do the things she would be doing now. You don't have to wait for the materialistic things now; it's the feelings you are feeling and the energy you are putting out. So, always go back to becoming self-aware, reprogramming your subconscious mind, and creating a routine and habits for your success which will all lead to attracting your dream clients and a life you desire to create. Let's make your dreams a reality! Check out my linktree to join my community, download your free workbook, and connect with me. Let's have a chat. I am here to guide you on your journey. Remember, you are worthy, and you are an unstoppable force.

## Heather Stokes Benton

CEO/Owner/Founder of Financial GPS

https://www.linkedin.com/in/heather-stokes-899624204/
https://www.facebook.com/HeatherStokesGetFinanciallyFit
https://www.instagram.com/heathersfinancialfocus/
https://www.facebook.com/groups/490021218981192

I am a wife, mother, homeschooler, and business owner. I am a giver, a motivator, and a developer, and I do not accept the answer no. I only see it as a challenge. My road to success has changed many times. Life has derailed my journey, and I have built a new path each time. I went to college for Forensic Psychology and worked for multiple government agencies over the next eight years. When I met my husband, he was a flight attendant and owned a limousine business. We lived a lavish life. 9/11 was our first major setback; three years later, he suffered a major injury and pancreatic cancer at 40. I could have given up, but with three girls depending on us, that was not an option. I had to learn how to be creative with money. Now it is my mission to help others to go from surviving to thriving. Being a mother and running a business can feel overwhelming at times. I find the key to keeping it all together is balance.

# BUILDING YOUR LEGACY

By Heather Stokes Benton

We have come a long way, but we can do better. A recent study showed that Millennial women are more likely to leave investment decisions to their husbands than any other age group. The surveys included nearly 1,700 married couples including heterosexual and same-sex couples. I find this extremely concerning because women are living longer than men. The average life expectancy for a woman is at least five years longer than a man's, not to mention divorce rates have doubled since the 90s, maybe even tripled following the pandemic. Given these two factors alone, 8 out of 10 women will end up alone and solely responsible for their families and their financial well-being. Therefore, a lack of knowledge of your financial situation or awareness can be catastrophic.

I have sat across the table from many women who are lost, overwhelmed, and stuck rebuilding. Nearly 60% of widows and divorcees said they wish they had been more involved in financial planning decisions with 56% of women discovering hidden debt, inadequate savings, or overly conservative or aggressive investments that affected their lifestyle and retirement goals.

It's not as if women aren't contributing funds or touching money. Most women are comfortable and savvy in handling the bulk of the day-to-day finances of the household and contribute half or more of the budget. But when it comes to planning for retirement or investment, there is a disconnect. I am not saying don't plan with your significant other. You both should be working toward a common goal. However, trusting and being led blindly into your future financial wellness with no checks and balances can lead to failure.

Gender roles are certainly hard to shake with men traditionally handling the long-term financial planning decisions instead of their wives. Men also tend to make more money than women, but even though they were the breadwinners, that reality has mostly changed. So, why are female or equal breadwinners still leaving financial decisions to their husbands? What I have found is that it is a lack of confidence.

We need to change our money mindset approach, let go of our old negative ideals, and develop a more positive relationship with money. No one, male or female, needs to be an expert to handle retirement and investment decisions. You just need to ask the right questions, gain basic financial literacy, engage in your finances, and take an active role.

Aside from deciding to take an active role in your financial wellness, you need to set goals and make a plan of action. Even though we may still live in a man-driven world, that does not mean we can't, as women, rise above social norms. After deciding to take an active role in building your legacy, you need to understand your FIN (Financial Independence).

This is not my first chapter or book, but it has been the most challenging. I have rewritten it several times. Finances, financial struggles, growth, and wellness are personal to my journey. It is my passion and has become my life's work. My name is Heather, and I am the owner and CEO of Financial GPS. I work with women and families to build financial security and generational wealth and secure their legacy. So many of us put our needs, wants, and money plans on the back burner. Why is this? What I have been guilty of, and I find many other women do, is putting everyone and everything else first and taking a back seat approach. We must stop doing this and leaving the financial decisions up to our male counterparts. We need to understand the importance of financial knowledge and our worth. This is still a struggle, even today, for many women. So, how can we work on building our legacy?

I am sure you are wondering what I am talking about. Your FIN is the amount you will need to retire or become independent from your current income. Everyone's FIN differs based on their needs, wants, and obligations. The rule of thumb is that *financial independence is when you save roughly 25 times your annual spending.* At this point, your finances are independent of your paycheck. Once you understand where you need to be, then we can decide where you want to be in the future.

Wealth Building is intentional and takes dedication. However, it is measurable and attainable, even in these challenging times! Be intentional about your finances by reviewing your spending and working off a budget; you'll have a clear idea of where your money is going. Find out where you can cut back on spending and where you can save. Cut it out! Once you've freed up some funds you didn't know you had, you can set effective financial goals like paying off debt, adding to your savings, securing your retirement, and growing that generational wealth to build your legacy.

A key factor in building a legacy is establishing the foundation for meeting our needs and achieving financial stability. Now we can discuss how to build residual income and develop a stronger future for your family, a better start for your children, and ensure generational wealth.

## Let's talk about how to ensure generational wealth while on your path to success.

Permanent life insurance efficiently maximizes the distribution of assets to a spouse, child, or charity. With the protection of a will or trust, life insurance can help increase the amount you pass on to heirs and organizations. Some people will tell me I don't have kids or a house; I don't need a will. The reality is that you need a will if you have an income, savings, debit, loans, or any type of financial situation (which is essentially everyone).

If you don't establish a will, the government has a plan called probate that will prevent your loved ones from accessing any of your assets and be responsible for your debits. Please get life insurance and an estate plan to protect your loved ones and your assets. Spare them the hassle and cost of fighting the courts and each other.

On a positive note, a life insurance policy ensures the goals you and your loved ones are working towards can still be accomplished even if you are not here. It allows you to leave an inheritance without your beneficiaries paying income tax on the money they receive. So, if you buy a policy with a $500,000 death benefit, your heirs will get $500,000. Therefore, life insurance is a good way to transfer wealth and provide instant generational wealth.

Now that we have taken an active role in our finances, established a plan, took action, and secured our financial wellness, how do you take that next step to build your legacy? I want you to take the next step as a family. A legacy involves passing on the finances, the business, the residual income, or real estate. So no matter what legacy it is, you have to educate the next generation on what they are getting, the benefits it offers, how to maintain it, and how to grow it. Otherwise, all your hard work was for nothing.

## Financial literacy starts at home. Your children are never too young to start or help out.

Find ways to introduce it in a fun way. Here are some ways to integrate financial literacy into activities with your kids at home. When they are little, they read age-appropriate stories about money, spending, and saving. As they get a little older, you can have a savings competition! Whoever saves the most can receive a bonus!

Set up a family savings jar and come up with a goal you're saving for, like a special trip or activity in the future. Consider using an allowance as a learning tool and letting them budget for their own toys.

Communication of goals at work, in your business, or as a family as they get older can be helpful. They can help you stay accountable for your actions, celebrate your success and support, and understand how to work through shortcomings or adjustments. This will help them prepare to handle success, finances, and conflict in the future.

Through a change in money mindset, taking an active role in your financial future, planning, taking actionable steps, securing wealth, encouraging financial literacy at home, and communicating, you are well on your way to building a legacy. We don't plan to fail, but we often fail to plan. You will see growth through faith in yourself, focus on your mission, and intentional actions. Sometimes the first step is admitting you don't know everything, which is ok. I was not always on the right plan. It takes humble, honest, and intentional actions to achieve financial wellness. It's like any other type of wellness; it takes work, but the benefits can be life-changing for yourself and those around you who outlive you.

I ask clients several questions that are typically the most effective and life-changing if they are brutally honest with themselves. First, when discussing generational wealth, I ask them to consider two things before developing their plan. Do you want to spoil your children as much as you can now and live a lavish life with them? Or, do you want first to secure yourself and their financial stability now and for generations to come?

Second, when discussing ensuring financial wellness during growth, you must ask yourself these questions. Do you want your family to have the same or better quality of life in the event that you are not here? What does that look like, and what does that mean? Often, individuals struggle with estate planning. The most effective way I plan with people is for them to imagine the worst has happened, and they are not here. What do the next three days look like? What about the next three months? What about the next three years? How do your children start in life without your support? How does your loved one retire without your joint income? How do you want to prepare for that?

Okay, now you have changed your mindset, improved your relationship with money, taken an active role in your finances, developed a plan, encouraged financial literacy, and ensured generational wealth. Make that money because you are strong, capable, and able to rise and conquer the world. Building your legacy is in your control. Look for a financial consultant, advisor, or coach with your interests at heart and with whom you can trust and have an open and honest conversation.

Remember that, like all wellness, it takes intention and work, but the benefit outweighs the sacrifice. I hope this chapter has helped motivate you, encouraged your journey to financial wellness, and made you feel that wealth-building is attainable. If you have questions, concerns, or need some guidance, please reach out and mention this book to get a complimentary Financial Needs Assessment to get you on your path to wellness! We are stronger together!

**Pamela Kurt**

Best Version of You LLC
Professional Women Networking and Life Coach

https://www.linkedin.com/in/pamela-kurt-41a26ba/
https://www.facebook.com/Best-Version-You-103772311530954
https://www.instagram.com/best_version_you
https://pamkurt.com/

Ms. Kurt is an attorney and owns Kurt Law Office LLC, with offices throughout northeast Ohio. She is very involved and won several community awards. She is also a best-selling author and public speaker. Her passion is to support and empower women to be the best they can be! The most personal enjoyment is when her clients find their own way. A new business as a professional women's life coaching practice has been born… BEST VERSION of YOU! This is an opportunity to elevate professional women to be the best version of themselves. Dream, Believe, and Achieve is her signature coaching program. Her coaching program has allowed her clients on a powerful self-discovery journey. She is currently accepting new private coaching clients and is available for speaking engagements. Please contact her at BestVersionYou.com or PamKurt.com to start your journey to become the BEST YOU!

# WORKING WITHOUT A NET

By Pamela Kurt

I have often stated publicly that I "work without a net." My reference is financial. I do not have a rich husband or family; I work for myself without a steady paycheck. I have been through some tough times financially. Some may not even know how good my "rob Peter to pay Paul" skills are finely tuned. I have done what I had to do to get through and make it.

I have had times when I took pennies to the gas station to get a quarter for the washing machine. Then I had to put my son's pants on a chair, hoping they dried overnight. And when they didn't, I used my hair dryer to finish the job. I would pray about money daily. I would worry about money daily. But, of course, I believe that the two can't both work. This has proved true to me. Finances, for me, is a mindset. Do I deserve it, do I need it, and do I get it? Do I believe it?

What I know is that I have gone through this life journey. I work without a net. My only safety net is God. This is the mindset for me to be who I am, where I am, and where I am going! As I mentioned, I don't have any guarantee of income. So, I try to live by common practices of being smart financially.

Best practices for managing your finances:

1. Create a budget
2. Cut down on unnecessary expenses and luxuries
3. Plan for the unexpected and have an emergency fund
4. Have a savings account
5. Don't go into debt; keep debt to credit ratio in proper standing

Oh, that all sounds great! BUT…

In my lifetime, it's hard to do any of that. I can create a budget and usually more bills than money even if I pay the minimums on the credit cards. I have cut down on "extras" from cable to generic brands for the household. Plan for the unexpected, then cars break down, and things break, but usually, this happens with more expense than saved funds. Have a savings account; that sounds great too. And we are told that as a child, keep your savings account. Oh, we are also told, "Don't go into debt but have some debt, not a lot but just enough," whatever that means. So I TRY to do all of the right things, but life happens. So, all of this advice and cliches sound great and might work for some, but they probably won't work for most.

I am here to say that I have been more than broke to have more than enough and then had to start all over again. But how do you keep the mindset to continue going? Through faith, my friends. God is always there, and while it may be sound advice to save money and spend sensibility, some of us have had times when it wasn't possible. So I pray and believe. I was recently reminded that I would also be ok.

During COVID, like many small businesses, my business was affected. One week during the shutdown, I received a check for $289; that was the entire week's income. I had a staff of three lawyers, four support staff, and a building at that time with four locations. We had to downsize the staff, the number of locations, etc. I was freaking out. I used my own money and resources to keep afloat. Yet during this time, courts were NOT shut down, and we were still expected to work by clients and courts even if it was only via Zoom or phone. But the money was a struggle since so many people were laid off, people were requesting an extension, couldn't pay bills, etc.

However, as usual, God was there for me. There were many stressful times, and I thought the worst was coming. But you know what? I learned how to rob Peter to pay Paul yet again. Now two years later, I am getting back on track. It was stressful for everyone, but if it weren't for my faith, I wouldn't have gotten through that financial time. Sometimes I felt quite defeated.

I know in my heart and soul that God will provide for me. That doesn't mean I think he's a genie, and I can make a wish. I use the tools provided and do what I can to make things happen. And continue to maintain my mindset. There is always enough. I am worthy, and I deserve it. I know that the more income and wealth, the more people I can help. It has taken me years to get that one. God takes care of me as long as I do my part. My part: pray, mindset, and do what I can do for myself! Sometimes that means learning, reaching out, and simply "robbing Peter to pay Paul" until it gets resolved.

There are many tools and resources available. This doesn't usually mean free money but ways to get business loans and payments. Ways to meet your cash flow needs and ways to continue your business. As I was learning and navigating this system, a few employees were laid off. Every day, I would be stressed about the financial commitment; I would pray daily, "Thy will be done!" It was HARD! But I needed to let things go, and things happened. There was some COVID relief via PPP loans, SBA loans, delayed payments, etc. I watched videos, webinars, and seminars daily to learn. The local Chamber of Commerce, SBA sites, and other entrepreneurs shared information as it was learned about the changes in law and the presentations and information created. All of the new and continually changing financial information was sometimes overwhelming. But I would use the resources I found and daily take on one challenge at a time. I kept on my patience and perseverance. There were days that I never thought we would have answers or I could make it. I keep thinking of so many families, from employees to clients, counting on me. Yet, I made it through only by my mindset and working without a net.

I look back, and my mindset was another God-given gift for me. God really showed the way daily. I would have never planned how all of the financial moves, and everything fell in place. Like many other business owners, it has taught me many new ways to do business. Most of the "new ways" were more efficient and cost-effective. I was also able to review budgets and numbers in a different light. As I say, I work without a net. I didn't have financial support. But I was given peace of mind to make the necessary decisions daily.

Going through this brought me back to basics; it taught me to slow down and practice my faith. I don't take finances for granted. Sometimes we get so overwhelmed or busy that we forget how blessed we are.

Keep the mindset and make a list of all debt/bills. How much would you need? How can you get it? Pray about it. Your direction will be shown. And let it go, BELIEVE! You will get through any financial problem with God. Keep the mindset. You too can work without a net. You are worthy and will always have enough. Don't forget to thank him for the opportunities, wealth, and overall abundance! You got this!

# JOIN THE MOVEMENT!
## #BAUW

## Becoming An Unstoppable Woman
## With She Rises Studios

She Rises Studios was founded by Hanna Olivas and Adriana Luna Carlos, the mother-daughter duo, in mid-2020 as they saw a need to help empower women worldwide. They are the podcast hosts of the *She Rises Studios Podcast* and Amazon best-selling authors and motivational speakers who travel the world. Hanna and Adriana are the movement creators of #BAUW - Becoming An Unstoppable Woman: The movement has been created to universally impact women of all ages, at whatever stage of life, to overcome insecurities, and adversities, and develop an unstoppable mindset. She Rises Studios educates, celebrates, and empowers women globally.

# Looking to Join Us in our Next Anthology or Publish YOUR Own?

She Rises Studios Publishing offers full-service publishing, marketing, book tour, and campaign services. For more information, contact info@sherisesstudios.com

We are always looking for women who want to share their stories and expertise and feature their businesses on our podcasts, in our books, and in our magazines.

## SEE WHAT WE DO

**OUR PODCAST**

**OUR BOOKS**

**OUR SERVICES**

Be featured in the Becoming An Unstoppable Woman magazine, published in 13 countries and sold in all major retailers. Get the visibility you need to LEVEL UP in your business!

Have your own TV show streamed across major platforms like Roku TV, Amazon Fire Stick, Apple TV and more!

Learn to leverage your expertise. Build your online presence and grow your audience with FENIX TV.
https://fenixtv.sherisesstudios.com/

Visit www.SheRisesStudios.com to see how YOU can join the #BAUW movement and help your community to achieve the UNSTOPPABLE mindset.

Have you checked out the *She Rises Studios Podcast?*

Find us on all MAJOR platforms: Spotify, IHeartRadio, Apple Podcasts, Google Podcasts, etc.

**Looking to become a sponsor or build a partnership?**

Email us at info@sherisesstudios.com

SHE RISES
STUDIOS

www.ingramcontent.com/pod-product-compliance
Lightning Source LLC
Chambersburg PA
CBHW071352120626
46546CB00002B/664